Contents

    Acknowledgements

    Introduction

1   **Simple Reality**   1
The Essence

2   **Worldview**   13
How Our Story Influences Our Experience Of Reality

3   **Afflictive Emotions, Attitudes, Beliefs And Values**   17
As A Surgeon Probes Deeply Into The Human Body To Promote Healing, We Must Understand The Inner Workings Of Our Personal Narrative And Identity To Attain A Sustainable Life Filled With Joy

4   **Identity**   22
Where We Think We Are Determines Who We Think We Are

5   **True Self And False Self**   26
Understanding The Distinction Between Who We Are And Who We Are Not, Empowers Us To Transcend The Illusion That Is The Foundation For All Human Suffering

6	**The Point Of Power Practice**	34
	Taking Complete Control Of Your Choices	
7	**Response And Reaction**	37
	Distinguishing Between Authentic And Illusory Power	
8	**Intuition And Intellect**	44
	Choose Carefully Which Of These Human Attributes Is Charting The Course Of Your Life	
9	**Feeling And Emotion**	46
	Transcendent Joy Lifts Us Beyond The Suffering Of Afflictive Emotion	
10	**Paradigm B**	53
	The Emotional Reactions, Beliefs, Attitudes And Values Of This Age-Old Story Explain The Human Condition	
11	**Paradigm A**	62
	By Embracing Our Authentic Power We Can Create A New Sustainable Human Community	
12	**Paradigm Shift**	73
	We Are All Born Into An Ongoing Story, But We Don't Have To Remain There	
13	**Meditation**	85
	Practicing Meditation, We Can Reveal Our True Identity And Profoundly Enhance Our Experience Of Life	

14	**Present Moment**	96
	We Have The Power To Transcend All Problems, All Suffering, All Delusion – We Are Free	
15	**Peak Experience**	106
	Simple Reality Is Our Natural State And Most Of Us Have Been There For At Least A Short Visit	
16	**Silence, Simplicity And Solitude**	110
	Becoming Quiet, Slowing Down And Spending Time Alone Can Be Transformational	
17	**Absolute And Relative**	114
	Understanding The Distinction Between Reality And Illusion Can Free Humanity From Our Ongoing Self-Destruction	
18	**Transcendence**	120
	We Must Increase Our Understanding Of Where We Are Going In The Paradigm Shift And The Obstacles To Getting There	
19	**Fear**	127
	Human Energy Has Been Used To Create A Fear-Driven Narrative But We Can Always Use That Energy To Express A Story Wherein Compassion Is The Dominant Human Expression	
20	**Compassion**	133
	The Most Fundamental And Authentic Human Behavior Is That Of Compassion	

21	**The Implicate Order**	136
	What Is The Source Of The Wisdom And Energy Which Connects All Of Creation And How Can We Use It?	
22	**The Algebra Of Simple Reality**	144
	Mystics Have Been Very Creative In Teaching Simple Reality	
23	**Right View**	148
	Experiencing Oneness, The Inter-Connection And Inter-Relatedness Of All Of Creation, Influences All Of Us To Treat Each Other And The Environment With Compassion	
24	**The Collective Unconscious**	155
	An Awareness Of Sub-Conscious Influences On Our Behavior Is Essential To The Attainment Of True Freedom	
25	**Buddha And Christ**	159
	Two Sides Of The Same Coin	
26	**Self-Reliance**	171
	Within Each Of Us Is Everything Necessary To Attain Our Highest Expression	
27	**Conditioning And Behavior Modification**	179
	True Freedom Involves Changing Our Deepest Conditioned Behaviors	

Appendix A - 6 Step Program	183
Appendix B – Dialogues	184
Appendix C – Glossary	187
Bibliography	199
Notes	208

Acknowledgements

To Carole Adams my friend and editor, for spotting the foggy bits, putting the periods where they belong, and patiently discussing and discussing and discussing the principles of Simple Reality without nodding off or at least not often. She continues to believe in me and has never waivered, not once.

To Kevin Bradshaw my dear friend who has the courage to demonstrate the principles of Simple Reality in his own life, moment by moment, day by challenging day. We continue to venture down the rabbit hole together into the magical world of truth and beauty.

To Jim Doherty my college roommate and lifelong buddy who encouraged me to break out of my cocoon and test my wings with this book. His expertise as a professional editor, publisher and agent was invaluable. As a trusted friend, I knew I could rely on his integrity, enthusiasm and encouragement.

To Linda LeBlanc who has been to the promised land of cyber-publishing and back, and continues to guide me over the river and through the woods.

To Tina and Lino Gonzales for listening, listening, and listening and with their compassion helped me transform my darkness into light.

To Kevin Todeschi my longtime and fun-loving friend, who is the Executive Director and CEO of Edgar Cayce's Association for Research and Enlightenment (A.R.E.), for inspiring me with his tireless dedication to human transformation and the ideal of Oneness.

My Sanga (meditation group) who listened to Simple Reality emerge over many years with unconditional love and support.

To my friends and family who, without judgment, allowed me to "go away" and "be silent" for these many years, so that I can learn and live the principles of Simple Reality.

To my fellow "team" members who in their courageous pursuit of truth revealed to "me" the truth of Simple Reality.

Introduction

Is it possible that the current human condition is a result of our being out of touch with reality, of not understanding the fundamental principles of how to live on this planet? What if many of the wisest poets, scientists, mystics and philosophers have said that this is the case? You might be interested in what they have said about how to be self-reliant, how to utilize the authentic power that lies within you and how to change your lifestyle to support a healthier, happier day-to-day experience of life. We are not talking about positive thinking, prayer or affirmations but permanent structural changes in consciousness that are transformational. They knew about these choices and now so can you.

In order to shift from the current human condition, an unsustainable paradigm B, to a sustainable paradigm A, a clear and profound distinction must be made between the two. A paradigm shift is not fundamentally a matter of intellectual comprehension but an "insight" involving your intuitive inner wisdom. We "feel" our way across the chasm between the old and the new narrative – we do not "think" our way in a logical, linear, sequential way from concept to increasingly complex concept. Please keep your intellect subordinate to your intuition—we already know this material—but most of us have not "felt" it for a very long time.

You will find that source numbers follow each quote. They refer to the notes for each chapter which are found at the end of the book.

Visit the *SIMPLE REALITY* blog at http://mysimplereality.com

Chapter One

Simple Reality: The Essence

This chapter is a synopsis of the fundamental principles that when understood and applied are transformational. Everything needed to begin the process that we could call a paradigm shift is contained in this chapter, including the blueprint on how to build a new lifestyle and the tools with which to do it. Subsequent chapters will deepen your understanding of the principles of Simple Reality, fleshing out the details that will support your new worldview, identity and behavior.

> *The unaware life is not worth living.*
> Socrates

This chapter can be characterized in three ways. First, as a prescription for a suffering humanity, secondly, as a synthesis of wisdom available since the beginning of time—that is to say human intuition as it has expressed itself over several millennia—or, third, it can simply be taken as a description of two realities. The common reality (life as usual), is the choice most of us have made. I label it paradigm B or P-B. It forms the basis of the global culture as we know it today. The other option is Simple Reality, which I have labeled paradigm A or P-A. It is known only to a relatively small number of people. Yes I did say "option" because every moment of every day all of us choose which reality we want to create and then we experience the consequences of that choice. Our experience tells us that it is possible for an individual or a group of people in an organization or even a nation to choose self-destructive behavior. In fact, it is today the dominant human behavior by far. But if the alternative is unknown to most people, it is easier to understand why most of humanity has chosen to create an unsustainable future instead of a sustainable one.

Once again, how effectively human communities or individuals function depends upon how well they understand reality. Given that the way humanity as a whole is living today is unsustainable, we must not have a very deep understanding of what reality is. This is very sad because the principles underlying P-A are not difficult to understand. What humanity needs is a more pragmatic approach to problem solving and less self-destructive behavior patterns. What humanity needs is a grasp of Simple Reality.

In a culture that values complexity, how do I expect anyone to believe that reality can be simple? Fortunately, we have a lot of support going back thousands of years that will help paint a vivid and compelling picture of a reality that is simple to create. Ironically, the major obstacles to our consideration of an alternative reality will include what we think we know and our ingrained conditioned behavior or "old habits" of both thinking and behaving. Simplicity itself has become a casualty of the human condition.

Much of what we think we know about reality is contained in our institutions and intellectual disciplines such as government, education, science, philosophy, psychology, and religion. Since most of us can agree that we have developed an unsustainable global village culture, we must admit that our institutions and knowledge have failed us. They have failed to give a profound response to what I call the Three Great Questions: Where am I? Who am I? and Why am I here? Human cultures were created out of a common human desire to give meaning to life, to answer the universal human questions. We will see why that didn't happen in this book.

A second major obstacle to understanding and creating Simple Reality has been language itself. As you will see in Simple Reality, we will not use the complex, metaphorical and ambiguous language often found in each of the aforementioned institutions and disciplines in order to understand, articulate, and practice Simple Reality. We will use a secular (not religious) language which is inclusive. We will use a simple psychological (not Freudian) language that is commonly understood. We will not use the technical and esoteric language of science because we are working at a more profound level beyond the scope of that discipline. And we will ignore the language of philosophy which, although intellectually challenging and enjoyable for many of us, has little relevance for Simple Reality. Simple Reality is profound, not complex.

Philosophers love to discuss how many angels can occupy the head of a pin? None! There are no angels. If you are unwilling to be your own angel—you are out of luck.

In the process of evolution, humanity has garnered a lot of knowledge and now it is time to become discriminating as to how to use that knowledge. We must learn to distinguish between what is useful in creating a sustainable future and what is not, between what works and what does not work. We may be amazed how little knowledge is actually needed to improve the human condition on planet earth.

And finally (if your teeth have not yet been rattled, this will do it), we must learn to rely on our intuition, not our intellect. The intellect is very useful but it must be subordinated to our own inner wisdom. We have been navigating using our intellectual charts for some time now, but we have hit an iceberg and we are sinking. It is time to change vessels to one that is seaworthy—to one that provides peace, freedom, joy, compassion and happiness to all human adventurers seeking profound answers to the Three Great Questions. It is time that we all shifted to the transcendent Good Ship Simple Reality. But of course, you may choose to stay on the Not So Good Ship Global Titanic—that's up to you.

Let us return to the importance of language again because we will be learning some critical words with very specific meanings as we look at both P-B and P-A. It is important that you use the connotation I assign regardless of what you previously understood the word to mean. I give words a very specific meaning within the context of P-B or P-A and those definitions will become increasingly clear as we use them. For example, what does paradigm mean? I use paradigm, worldview, story, narrative and context as synonyms which mean an individual's or a collective's feelings, beliefs, attitudes, and values. In other words your worldview would be your response to the question: *Where am I?* or an alternative form of that question such as: *What is the nature of reality?*

The Story of Self-Destruction (Paradigm B)

As "modern" human beings, we pride ourselves on being able to solve problems when in reality we cannot even distinguish problems from symptoms. Because of this we waste our energy chasing our tails—creating policies that only make matters worse—and which obscure the very reality that would illuminate a sustainable future.

> *We lay waste our power*
> *Getting and spending*
> *Little we see in nature that is ours*
> *We have given our hearts away.*
>   Wordsworth

For example, the so-called "war on drugs" in the United States assumes that the producers, transporters or distributors of drugs are the problem. The solutions then would seem to be eradication, interdiction and criminalization. We often support totalitarian governments and pay them to seek out and destroy the relevant crops and sometimes the farmers and villagers as well. We chase speedboats and airplanes and try to detect balloons full of cocaine in the stomachs of human "mules". We impose prison sentences on both distributors and users sometimes with overtones of racial or socio-economic prejudice.

Since the "supply" side is only a symptom of the real problem, none of the aforementioned solutions work. We have failed to see reality. The "demand" on the part of Americans is the place to start looking for the real problem. A good question to ask would be: *Why do so many Americans want to engage in self-destructive behavior?* The answer to this question would help us understand what the real problem is and to begin formulating effective policies for the "war on drugs." Until then we will continue to go in circles wondering why we are so frustrated and confused and why our policies are so absurdly ineffective.

This book will answer the question above and all others that must be realistically addressed if we are to avoid the deepening insanity that has become "life as usual" for the people of the global village.

We have the choice to create for ourselves a radically different future than the one we have chosen. If we don't change our behavior we are faced with a modern version of the Four Horsemen of the Apocalypse. We all have our own description of the perfect storm building on the horizon. We fear global warming, over-population, pandemics, environmental degradation, nuclear winter, domestic violence, terrorists, organized crime, economic collapse and on and on. Again, all of these events, if they occur, will be merely symptomatic of unconscious choices made by each of us in our everyday lives. Let's see what those choices have been in more detail.

First, as individuals, we are all born into an ongoing story. As we pull back for a moment to look at ourselves in the bigger picture, we can see that our story (our answer to the question: *Where am I?*) has determined our identity (*Who am I?*) and that our identity has driven our behavior (*What should I do, now that I know where and who I am?*). Each human being is actively engaged (mostly unconsciously) in answering The Three Great Questions as they live out their lives.

We can see how critically important it is to choose a profound paradigm because all of human experience flows from that choice. Remember, our story determines our identity which drives our behavior. A fundamental goal in shifting to P-A is to change our behavior. If we fail in that, we have merely been engaged in an intellectual exercise and we have already begun to understand what a waste of time that is. I am going to be repetitive throughout this book because we must internalize the fundamental principles of Simple Reality by repeating them until they replace those mistaken assumptions that we have grown used to. These principles are profound and critical to our process.

The Three Great Questions—chew these up and digest them:
- Where am I? (What is the nature of reality?)
- Who am I? (What is my identity?)
- Why am I here? (What is the meaning of life and how am I to behave?)

THE STORY THAT DOESN'T WORK (PARADIGM B)

Where am I?

In the P-B narrative we are taught to believe that we are distinct and separate from other human beings, and from the forms and "forces" of nature (our physical environment) and from God (if we are religious). This belief in separation causes us to fear other people, nature and God. We live in a constant state of existential anxiety. We do not feel safe in P-B and the only way out is to die, but alas we also fear death. In P-B we tend to live our lives in the past, experiencing shame and guilt for our past actions or in longing for an experience that is irretrievably gone. Or we live in the future, craving status, wealth or other illusory attainments, most of which won't come to pass, and if they do, they don't bring the satisfaction we had anticipated.

Fear of other people enables us to rationalize hatred and violence, fear of nature causes environmental destruction, and fear of God supports self-hatred and both physical and psychological self-destruction. We live in a shattered and fear-driven story and there is no way to make it work. We must find another one.

Who am I?

Because we have a fragmented narrative in P-B we also have a segmented identity. We identify with our physical body, our emotions and even the flow of thoughts in our mind as well as the forms in our physical world, including other people. We patch together a pseudo-identity. Let's take a look beneath the surface of this dysfunctional human identity and see what makes it tick.

We are all born with three fundamental needs which we can label as security, sensation and power. Our very survival, beginning at birth, depends on how well these basic needs are provided for, therefore, each of us must create what is often called a survival strategy. The energy that drives most of our behavior flows from these three "energy centers" and they form the basis of our identity in P-B.

Interestingly enough, three American cities provide an analogy for each of these drives and will make it easier for us to remember the behavioral characteristics of each.

The Security Center—New York City and Wall Street

The basic belief behind the security energy center is that we can guarantee our security (which begins most fundamentally with obtaining food, clothing and shelter) and assuage our existential anxiety, by accumulating material things. This drive can never be satisfied no matter how big a pile of "stuff" we manage to collect. This part of our identity, combined with the context of P-B, has us believing that we must be very competitive to get our share of a limited amount of material wealth. Hence, we see other people or other nations as a threat and we project on them our deepest fears relating to our survival.

The Sensation Center—Las Vegas

This energy center is very complex since we are always seeking sensations, including esteem and affection, and "love" in its many forms. All human behaviors related to the problem of addiction are contained in the sensation energy center. Addictions fall into two categories—substance addictions and process addictions. Examples of each are alcoholism and gambling. The best we can do most of the time is escape from our suffering into our many additive behaviors or into the illusion of love. Now I want to go watch a soap opera!

The Power Center—Washington D.C.

The behavior that is driven by this energy center involves trying to control people or situations, promoting our status in society, enhancing our self-image, increasing our influence, working to add to our list of accomplishments, approval seeking, and promoting others' dependence on us. Of course, all three of the false-self energy centers are driven by fear. These fear reactions have been with us since before we climbed down from the trees and we continue to fear what we cannot control. And in truth we cannot control anything "out there" so we better give up the identity that needs to try to do that.

Why am I here?

In P-B no one has offered a profound or truly logical answer as to why we are here on this planet. The striving for security, sensations and power is ultimately unsatisfying and meaningless. We also seem to be outgrowing our religion-based myths and identities. Do we have to finish the story we started (P-B) even though the ending is too horrible to contemplate, or do we have another choice?

THE STORY THAT WORKS (PARADIGM A)

> *Who looks outside*
> *dreams.*
> *Who looks inside*
> *awakens.*
>   C. G. Jung

Where am I?

I want to repeat a question that we have already considered in the context of P-B. Is the paradigm that humanity has chosen sustainable? At this point we probably have almost universal agreement because most of us are coming to realize, however reluctant we are to think about it, that we cannot continue to behave as we are without creating greater and greater human suffering. Perhaps the reason that we don't want to think about our unfolding collective reality is that we feel impotent when faced with the enormity of the problems. We are not. We are making one big mistake, however, and that is creating a reality with problems that will grow increasingly beyond our ability to solve. We are continuing to perpetuate a narrative that is literally suicidal. Is there any good news concerning our situation? Yes, indeed. We had the power to create this story and we have the power change it. May I offer P-A – a healthy, sustainable alternative to P-B. Please notice how simple P-A is compared to P-B.

The fundamental reality of P-A is Oneness. All of creation is inter-related and inter-dependent. All of those persons and events that seem to offend me *are* me. The "other" is an illusion found only in P-B, which is also an illusion. The natural environment that nourishes me and provides me with air to breathe and water to drink, and that nourishes my body, mind and soul—*I am THAT*. I am not only one *with* all creation, I *am* all of creation – *I am THAT*. In P-A, I no longer choose to live in the illusion of being separate from nature and other people, alienated from my true self.

Who Am I?

What is our true identity? We were all born with an interior wisdom, often referred to as the "still, small voice", which will guide us, if we can hear it. We can hear our intuitive, inner wisdom only when we are in the present moment. The likelihood increases that we will be in the present moment when we practice these behaviors:

Simplicity + Silence + Solitude = Serenity (present moment)

We can also refer to this interior self as the "true self." It is what is referred to in the statement, "*I am THAT*." Our true self is beyond the ego, the false self or any sense of a separate "I" or "me." In the present moment, the true self is detached from craving and aversion and has no desire to have, know or do anything. It is profoundly free. Our true identity has no history, and no process of becoming, it simply *is*.

Therefore, it can only be "felt" when all false-self pursuits cease. When we become present, we automatically have attained our true identity as we shall see in the next section.

Why Am I Here?

How does one move from P-B to P-A, what is the discipline, what is the "practice"? To answer these questions, let's use an example of a common grievance among automobile drivers in the U.S.—being "cut off" in traffic. Notice how the context influences the interpretation of reality that I as the aggrieved person experience.

In P-B the offender may be unaware of what was done or may have intentionally, in anger, anxiety or frustration, moved abruptly in front of me. I, the "innocent victim," at this point have been triggered and begin to react with an afflictive emotion, usually anger or fear. That emotion can then be prolonged and reinforced by a physical or verbal "reaction" or by beginning a story in my mind. At the point of reaction I have indeed become a victim, not of the offending driver but of my own choice, consciously or unconsciously choosing to remain in the conditioned environment of P-B.

What is important to understand is that the offending driver in the scenario above, regardless of his/her motivation, has nothing to do with my reaction and is totally powerless to affect the story I'm creating in my mind. By reacting, I have defaulted to the habitual realm of suffering, the self-created story of self-inflicted pain and self-destruction, which could last anywhere from a few minutes to years or even decades. Madness would not be too strong a term to characterize this behavior.

In 2006 on C-470, the southwest portion of the beltway encircling Denver, near where I live, a man in an act of road-rage "cut-off" two men that he felt had disrespected him and then braked in front of them. Swerving to avoid contact, the second driver rolled his car and he and his passenger were both killed. The unrepentant "victim" was given a long prison sentence. Such are the all-too common fruits of imagined insults and the resulting reactions in the world of P-B.

Now let's take the same scenario used in the example above and substitute "response" for "reaction" at what I call "the point of power." That moment is a point in time where I can breathe and choose not to react or unconsciously give in to the conditioning of my false-self survival strategy.

In my life, I can always choose to have control (power) over my reactions. The power and responsibility is all mine and "the point of power"—that moment where I claim my power or give it away—is where I choose to react or respond. Beginning where I have been triggered and have the awareness of what is happening, I choose to relax, breathe and not react. In other words I claim the power of choice and do not physically, emotionally or mentally perpetuate a reaction (an afflictive emotion). With practice, and I have ample opportunity to practice this every day, the afflictive energy will subside. Once the afflictive energy melts away, I feel compassion for all involved, including myself, and I also "feel" the freedom and joy of the present moment.

Just as we made a distinction between "reaction" and "response," we can use the two words "emotion" and "feeling" to distinguish the sensations experienced in P-B and P-A. It's important to realize that the experiences of P-B and P-A are mutually exclusive. When I am behaving unconsciously in P-B, I will experience the "afflictive emotions" resulting from my "reactions." In P-A, I will experience the "feeling" of the present moment resulting from my ability to breathe, relax and "respond."

When we fall prey to the illusion of P-B, we find ourselves in continuous resistance to what is happening. Nothing works or gives satisfaction or happiness in this paradigm. The underlying source of energy in P-B is fear. In our complex behavioral strategies to deny reality, we behave as sleepwalkers in a nightmare. Obviously the goal is to wake up—choosing to not react at the "point of power" over and over again, day in and day out—staying present to reality no matter what that reality is. This is the process of "shifting" from the doomed Global Titanic to the Good Ship Simple Reality. This is the practice of waking up and living in the present moment which is the only "time and place" that life occurs.

Living in Simple Reality (being present) effectively prevents any form of self-destructive behavior among people or towards the environment. In other words, P-A is a sustainable paradigm. We have been led to believe that entering the present moment is complex and difficult and takes time, when indeed it is simple and relatively easy and involves no time and no process beyond The Point of Power Practice.

Do we have the courage and desire to wake up, to surrender to the freedom, joy, happiness, compassion and serenity of the perfect Now?

Which reality makes sense to you: P-B or P-A?

It's your choice. Climb into the lifeboat. You may not be able to see it clearly but through the fog only a short distance away is the Good Ship Simple Reality. I know because I've been there and so have you.

Chapter Two

Worldview

How Our Story Influences Our Experience Of Reality

Our worldview as individuals or as a collective (nation or global village) is all important. It is that story that determines how the creative energy in each person or collective is expressed. The energy that fuels the universe in and of itself is neutral. But the dominant narrative, the context we create that contains the neutral energy, tends to influence whether that energy is expressed in either a predominantly positive or predominantly negative way. If the human story were P-A, we would be compassionate human beings creating heaven on earth. However, since our story is P-B, even though many of us are kind, loving and passionately creative people, the dominant experience is the unsustainable madness that we encounter each and every day.

Obviously, we must begin to have a dialogue about how to change our story, how to shift the paradigm. That dialogue continues in this chapter around the topic of worldview. Hear what our venerable sages have to say about it. Internalize this perennial wisdom and begin The Point of Power Practice that can alter your experience of life.

A good working definition of worldview would be that it is comprised of feelings/emotions, beliefs, attitudes and values. To emphasize the importance of at least one of these components we have only to quote Bob Larzelere. "Beliefs completely determine your reality when held as the truth."[1] It is our worldview that determines whether the energy of a given experience is used to perpetuate suffering or is used for attaining present moment awareness, for waking up. Seth, channeled by Jane Roberts, is only too glad to affirm this aspect of Simple Reality. "Your social structure, from the largest metropolis to the smallest farm, from the wealthiest areas to the poorest ghettos, from the monasteries to the prisons, reflects the inner situation of the individual self and the personal beliefs that each of you hold."[2] Therefore, if humanity is to move from an unsustainable community to a sustainable one, our worldview individually, and collectively, is where we must begin our process of change.

"Worldviews, and the ways of knowing that produce and sustain them, structure our perceptions and define how we experience ourselves in relation to the universe. They determine how we relate to each other and to the Earth itself, how we find satisfaction, and how we come to terms with ultimate questions of living and dying. For these reasons, there is no matter of greater significance than which worldview, or paradigm, is ascendant in our society."[3]

Amen to that! The quote was from John E. Mack found in the Institute of Noetic Sciences, *The 2008 Shift Report.* As we learned in chapter one, our worldview determines our identity, our identity determines our behavior, and our behavior on this planet today needs radical change.

A worldview such as P-B can be very limiting and suffocating as well as self-destructive, as psychologist C. G. Jung was well aware. "But all those contents that refuse to fit into this whole are either overlooked and forgotten or repressed and denied."[4] The content of our life's experience that is repressed ends up in the shadow, and the denied portion haunt us in our dreams because the energy that underlies our story (P-B) is fear.

Humanity today tends to mistakenly think that we have made progress throughout history, particularly since the Industrial Revolution. That "progress" is very shallow and based on illusion. Our hubris is unjustified as Jung again reminds us. "Thus through what sociologist Levy-Bruhl has termed the 'participation mystique,' primitive man is contained physically and psychically in his world. In contrast, civilized man believes that he is separate from nature and in possession of an individual soul. Thus modern man must deprive nature of psychic reality and, in order to see his world objectively, deny all his archaic projections."⁵   Jung has reminded us of two profound principles that are foundational to a healthy worldview founded on Oneness. First, we are not separate from nature or anything else for that matter since all of creation is interdependent and interrelated. Secondly, there is no separate ego, no "I" or "me."

"But today," says Carter Phipps, "we know that the defining characteristics of our postmodern age, an era that was being born even as Jung lay dying, are its lack of a coherent worldview and its hostility toward any larger vision or 'metanarrative' that could help unify our society and give us the energy and perspective to respond to the problems and potentials of our time in history....a powerful coherent worldview that can allow us to thrive in a complex, globalizing, rapidly changing planetary culture."⁶

Phipps continues describing the contributions of the mystic and Jesuit priest, Pierre Teilhard de Chardin, which support our basic contentions concerning the importance of our worldview. "Our concepts and beliefs about life and reality, what he called our *a priori* convictions, tend to condition our experience. Indeed, these convictions help form powerful interpretive frameworks, worldviews that reflect our deepest conclusions about the nature of ourselves and the universe we live in. And because these worldviews are so primary, so fundamental, they affect everything else—how we think about family, community, politics, economics, religion, even spiritual experience..."⁷

We have talked about the belief portion of the worldview. What about values? Rollo May addresses values in his book *Man's Search for Himself*. "The belief in individual competition [seeking power] and reason [the intellect] we have been discussing are the ones which in *actuality* have guided modern Western development, and are not necessarily the ideal values."⁸

May seems to feel that without the anchor of P-A, human beings have been aimlessly drifting at sea. "...man's anxiety, bewilderment and emptiness—the chronic psychic diseases of modern man—occur mainly because his values are confused and contradictory, and he has no psychic core."[9]   Clearly, if we continue to depend on the beliefs and values of P-B, we are in serious trouble.

Just as a worldview explains the suffering of an individual, it also explains the experience of families, tribes and nations. A nation's worldview (P-B) is a myth specifically constructed to prevent a paradigm shift. "*The Epic of Gilgamesh* belongs to that group of Ancient Near Eastern myths which may be termed 'societal.' Each nation has its societal myth to justify and sustain functions: to validate prevailing social patterns, to provide rules and acceptable models for living, to supply divine sanction for the existing power structure, and to prove to the individual that the laws and customs of his country were superior of those of other countries. Thus the myth served the purpose of preserving the *status quo*."[10]

It is that status quo, that worldview, which we must all challenge with every ounce of energy within us.

In the next chapter, a more detailed look at the components of our worldview will deepen our understanding of why it is critically important to begin the dialogue about why and how we can begin retelling the human story.

Chapter Three

Afflictive Emotions, Attitudes, Beliefs And Values

As a Surgeon Probes Deeply Into the Human Body to Promote Healing, We Must Understand the Inner Workings of Our Personal Narrative and Identity to Attain a Sustainable Life Filled With Joy

Afflictive Emotions

> *Be not hasty in thy spirit to be angry: for anger resteth in the bosom of fools.*
> Ecclesiastes 7:9

All emotions are afflictive, that is to say, all emotions are expressions of human suffering. Examples of afflictive emotions are:

Alienation	Anger	Anxiety	Confusion
Blame	Boredom	Defeat	Depression
Despair	Doubt	Grief	Guilt
Jealousy	Loneliness	Longing	Pain
Panic	Regret	Remorse	Resignation
Shame	Romantic love	Shock	Sentimentality
Uncertainty	Stress	Terror	Unhappiness
Worry			

Afflictive emotions are fundamentally only energy. They originate outside of present moment awareness. Or to say it another way, awareness and afflictive emotions are mutually exclusive.

Fear is the primal energy foundational to all afflictive emotions. Environmental, cultural and personal differences provide the individual mind with the occasions to fragment that energy into different colorations to fit each individual. But let me repeat this all-important truth that we must confront in order to gain our freedom: the details of human suffering are unique to each individual—the cause is universal—it is fear.

Afflictive energy and its labels are a cultural creation and are basic elements within the story of that culture. For example, the four "humours" was the name given to a basic typology of afflictive energy during the Middle Ages:

> phlegmatic—unemotional and of a sluggish temperament
> melancholic—sadness or depression; gloomy or subject to sullenness
> sanguine—cheerful, confident, and passionate
> choleric—easily angered, bad-tempered; showing or expressing anger

You might ask why "cheerful, confident and passionate" (romantic love) should be included in the list of afflictive emotions. To be able to answer that question, we must understand the distinction between **feeling** and **emotion** which is the subject of a later chapter in this book. From the perspective of P-A, we can understand what Buddhists have come to realize and that is "'*All emotions are painful.*' This is something that only Buddhists would talk about. Many religions worship things like love with celebration and songs, Buddhists think, 'This is all suffering.'"[1] The good news is that when we are in the present moment (Now), afflictive emotions are absent and only feelings are experienced.

In the overly complex storyline of P-B we can get lost in a haze of emotional reaction. We cannot, for example, understand why some of our personal relationships are such a mess. Seth describes some of the confusion that is possible and reveals why a shift in perspective would be very helpful. "Hatred always involves a painful sense of separation from love, which may be idealized. A person you feel strongly against at any given time upsets you because he or she does not live up to your expectations. The higher your expectations the greater any divergence from them seems. If you hate a parent it is precisely because you expect such love. A person from whom you expect nothing will never earn your bitterness.... The hatred is meant to get you your love back. It is supposed to lead to a communication from you, stating your feelings—clearing the air, so to speak, and bringing you closer to the love object. Hatred is not the denial of love, but an attempt to regain it, and a painful recognition of circumstances that separate you from it..."[2] If our relationships existed in the context of P-A, they would be much simpler and therefore more wholesome because they would be based on feelings not emotions.

Most of us have experienced the water "mirage" or illusion of standing water that appears to be ahead of us on the highway as we drive across Kansas, for example, on a hot day in July. As we approach the mirage, it eventually disappears. We have been deceived by our senses. So it is in P-B. The fear that produces our afflictive emotion is like the mirage. We are frightened by that which seems to exist but upon closer examination, has no substantial reality. Every human problem and all the reactions that accompany it grow out of our reluctance to face our fears, to stay with them long enough to understand their fundamental nature. If we remain calm and patient as we sense the arising afflictive emotion and choose response over reaction, our anxiety and suffering will begin to fade like the mirage on a hot Kansas highway.

Attitudes

Attitude is another component of worldview, and can be defined as a state of mind or emotional reaction. I have called it an emotional reaction because in P-B it is often irrational with no basis in reality. To illustrate my point, let us take the British people and their reactions in a recent survey. All of humanity lives in the same fundamental reality but with widely varying relative attitudes. Americans in response to recent surveys that I have read are basically optimistic—not so the Brits.

"Even though they live in times of relative prosperity, a quarter of Britons surveyed agreed they face a 'hopeless future,' and one in three feels 'downright miserable.' The survey was conducted by the popular British health web site, NetDoctor. Ten percent said they would be better off dead.

"More than 400 men and women were asked to answer 80 questions online about their emotional health and what they thought of life. A quarter of those questioned said life was unfair, and more than 10 percent said they felt they had been dealt a miserable lot and that they were powerless to do anything about it."[3]

Because of the negative attitudes that prevail in P-B, we often assume a "victim" identity as seen above. We also, of course, feel powerless because in P-B, we are powerless. Until we embrace Simple Reality as our context, assume a new identity, and learn to use The Point of Power Practice, we will have a reactive attitude whether we are British or not.

Beliefs

Belief is a component of worldview and can be defined as something believed or accepted as true, especially a particular tenet or a body of tenets accepted by a group of persons. Hence, P-B is a belief. However, as Seth states, "You are not at the mercy of the past, or of previous convictions, unless you *believe* that you are. If you fully comprehend your *power* in the present [P-A], you will realize that action at that point also alters the past, its beliefs and your reactions."[4] It is important to add that we are also not at the mercy of the collective unconscious (our society's worldview) when we are in the present moment.

Values

> *It is essential that the student acquire an understanding of and lively feeling for values. He must acquire a vivid sense of the beautiful and of the morally good. Otherwise he, with his specialized knowledge more closely resembles a well-trained dog than a harmoniously developed person.*
> Albert Einstein

Value is a component of worldview and can be defined as a principle, standard, or quality considered worthwhile or desirable. Values are created when we choose our worldview, since our worldview determines our identity. In P-A, we will value compassion and Oneness because they will be foundational to our belief system. Self-destructive behaviors will no longer make sense and will gradually fade away as the values of P-A (Simple Reality) support response instead of reaction.

Chapter Four

Identity

Where We Think We Are Determines Who We Think We Are

We must be highly motivated, clear and focused in our dialogue about the importance of changing our worldview because we know that it determines our individual and collective identity/identities. When we are born it is as though we are handed a script that has us playing a character reading the lines of a fairytale character. We are expected to conform to that role and dutifully read our lines in response to the other characters on the stage of P-B. The penalties of failing to play our part exactly as written can be harsh.

The goal of Simple Reality as a "program" is designed to change human behavior, and since it is our identity that drives our behavior, it follows that understanding the dynamics of identity is critically important. To that end, we consult many wise people who have thought deeply about the relationship between behavior and identity.

> *The true nature of anything is the highest it can become.*
> Aristotle

Identity is the experience of oneself in relation to the world. Our identity is our destiny because it determines our behavior. The process of building a survival strategy, the fruitless pursuit of security, sensation, and power, results from "who" we "think" that we are, not the result of who we really are, as we shall see. As Sakyong Rinpoche states so clearly: "Running around trying to alleviate our suffering obscures our true nature—basic goodness—which is clear and unchanging…. The wisdom and love beneath the clutter of negativity are natural and permanent."[1]

How does P-B in general dictate one's identity? The self tries to align the forms of the outside world with the self-image. Starting with the parents, then other family and community members, peers and on out to the surrounding culture in general, one seeks to align the identity with the exterior "reality." A great deal of energy will be expended to accomplish this and failure to do so can lead to maladjustment and despair.

Many of us will experience the illusion that we have created a satisfactory adjustment to life in P-B but it will, over time, ultimately be unsustainable and unsatisfactory. Jungian Analyst, Dr. Edward Edinger, sheds light on this interesting relationship between illusory satisfaction in P-B and a more profound identity. "It is possible to be related, indeed lovingly related, to a particular religion, church or religious community without being contained in it. *Containment* is an unconscious phenomenon of psychic identification. One can be contained in a religion just as one can be contained in a family or other collective group. One then has no individual, living relation to the numinous archetypes. *Relatedness* to a religion, however, means connecting with it out of one's individual numinous experience. In the latter case we have not a community of believers, but rather a community of knowers, or better, a community of individuals, each of whom is a carrier of the living experience of the Self."[2] An experience of the Self is the "feeling" experienced in the present moment. Therefore, a conventional P-B identity must be transcended in order to "attain the highest" that we can become.

Once again let's look at the self-destructive nature of materialism or identifying with "things" [security] or status [power] in the community. Robert Powell was referring to this when he wrote: "Thus, the discovery of what one *is* must mean the very opposite of fostering one's sense of belonging, because it is a return to a state of total aloneness or Nothingness and thereby the destruction of all security."[3] The only true freedom and the related self-reliance comes from ceasing to identify with the false self energy centers and putting out the fire of our old conditioning (the craving of security, sensation, and power) by refusing to feed it any longer.

Attaining a profound identity is less a process of attaining something as it is getting rid of something—dis-identification. During the process of Vipassana (Insight meditation) one is taught to dis-identify with emotions, thoughts and the body (body sensations). As challenging as that is, one still has to further dis-identify with the ego (no "I"), all form (everything is impermanent) and ultimately with suffering. Suffering of course exists but one must accept life as it is and in doing so transcend the ever-present "unsatisfactoriness" of life. In a profound meditation practice one will become the observer of all reaction and thus attain freedom from all craving and aversion.

What often happens during meditation and what makes this practice so difficult for a beginner is identifying with body, mind and emotions. When we identify with our body we create the suffering associated with aches, pains, itches and all other physical sensations "pleasant" or "unpleasant." All sensations are suffering because they become the occasion for craving and aversion. When we identify with the mind we subject ourselves to the suffering of the compulsive, neurotic and endless fear-driven storyline. When we identify with our emotions we are in an almost constant reactive state characterized by fear, anger, jealousy, paranoia, and on and on ad infinitum. It requires a strong commitment to sit (in meditation) through these experiences but the payoff is worth it.

A shift in identity is possible during meditation as one becomes the "observer" of one's experience and stops identifying with the body, mind and emotions. Becoming the observer is an example of response instead of reaction. Creating consciousness (awareness) in this way leads to enhanced power and freedom. This higher level of awareness has many practical benefits such as dealing with phobias as described by Edward Edinger: "The ability to turn an unconscious complex which has one by the throat into an object of knowledge is an extremely important aspect for increasing consciousness... it is as though one who was fighting for his life in the arena were magically transported to the position of spectator—desperate reality becomes an image for contemplation, and the subject as 'knower' is removed beyond harm."[4]

Transcending P-B is the result of a profound meditation practice and should be the ultimate goal of any meditation, regardless of what intermediate benefits are realized. To stop a meditation practice before the "shift" to an observer consciousness is attained, before a new identity is realized, is to abort one's journey before the destination is reached.

The teachings of all sages emphasize the importance of shifting identities and seeing reality from that new perspective. Jesus said to his disciples in Chapter 95 in the Acts of John: "A mirror am I to thee that perceivest me." Edward Edinger explains that "In this text, Jesus is instructing the disciples how to separate subject from object, how to perceive experience as a mirror that provides an image of meaning rather than as chaotic anguish. This corresponds to active imagination or meditative reflection [response] which can turn an oppressive mood [reaction] into an object of knowledge by discovering the meaningful image imbedded in the mood."[5]   What Edinger is describing here is, in fact, The Point of Power Practice.

> *The game is not about becoming somebody, it's about becoming nobody.*
> Baba Ram Dass

This is perhaps the most challenging of the profound teachings of the mystics regarding identity. There is no "me," no "I," no separate identity that we commonly think of as the human personality. There is not even an "ego" around which the human personality is constellated in P-B. All of this is part of the ultimate illusion of the deluded human mind which as we have learned has no substantial reality.

True freedom can only be possible when we internalize the truth that we are not an ephemeral human body, mind or emotion-driven animal. We are pure energy, indestructible and existing in the eternal Now, beyond the confines of time and space. Jesus speaking in *A Course in Miracles* says, "…no trace remains of dreams of spite in which you dance to death's thin melody…. And then the Voice is gone, no longer to take form but to return to the eternal Formlessness of God."[6]

We are pure energy, beyond suffering and anxiety. That is our true identity.

Chapter Five

True Self And False Self

Understanding The Distinction Between Who We Are And Who We Are Not, Empowers Us To Transcend The Illusion That Is The Foundation For All Human Suffering

By constructing the survival strategy, which is itself an illusion, we are trying desperately to avoid the very thing that we are looking for. Due to our frantic having, doing, and knowing, and by our identification with the body, emotions and mind, we create the fog of mindless activity and a cloudy identity that obscures our natural state. The experience of our "true self" can only occur in the uncluttered clarity of Simple Reality.

The True Self

The true self is the shy, still small voice heard in contemplative silence. It is what is referred to in the statement "I am That." It is beyond the ego and any sense of a separate "I" or "self." It is timeless and eternal. It has always been and always will be. It exists in the present moment or the Absolute, and is not found in the relative (P-B) nor in the past or future. The true self is detached from craving and aversion and has no desire to have, know or do anything. It is profoundly free. The true self has no history, and no process of "becoming" because it simply *is.* Therefore it can only be "felt" when all processes cease.

> *Empty yourself and see that I am God!*
> Psalm 45:11

Karen Malik says that: "Essence [true-self] is the pure unconditioned nature of who we are—the purest fiber of our being. It is more fundamental and intrinsic than our personality....It is a permanent abiding presence....Essence is our true nature. It is being without the distortion of our personal history... When we lose contact with the experience and presence of our essence and its essential qualities, we literally feel a hole or emptiness or deficiency in ourselves. Most often this is frightening and painful. One of the characteristics of the ego/personality is that it feels it must compensate for this loss."[1] Unfortunately, that compensation occurs in the creation of the false self.

The False Self

The false self is ultimately an illusion. It is external, the self of "form," the "I," the ego, the unconscious, the collective unconscious and the shadow. The false self expends its energy in seeking security, sensation and power. It exists in the realm of the relative. The false self needs gods and gurus, religion and refuge, prayers and potions, *tantra* and teachings, myths and mysteries to perpetuate its existence. Until all these illusory emotions, beliefs, attitudes, values and activities are abandoned for the joy of the Now, we will be dominated and mesmerized by the false self.

"The ego," says Malik, "feels it can create its own strength, its own love, its own security—whatever it needs. However the compensations it uses only mimic the essential qualities, and rather than originating from essence, they are rooted in defensive avoidance of life's pain."[2] The Buddha discovered this 2,500 years ago, and stated it in the First Noble Truth (Life is Suffering), but the rest of us have yet to grasp what he was talking about even though he spent 45 years teaching many of the basic principles of Simple Reality.

Failure to acknowledge the existence of the false self and the role it plays in human suffering keeps us trapped in P-B. Jung proved that he understood this to some degree when he said: "The more that consciousness is influenced by prejudices, errors, fantasies, and infantile wishes, the more the already existing gap will widen into a neurotic dissociation and lead to a more or less artificial life, far removed from healthy instincts, nature and the truth."[3]

The individual false self is influenced by and is, in fact, a part of the collective false self of humanity in general. Jung's collective unconscious, what Ernest Holmes called "race thought" plays a key role in P-B and in humanity's self-destructive behavior. "Few people are able to escape the pernicious effects of these unconscious suggestions and race thought 'hypnotizes everyone from the cradle to the grave.'"[4]

To put it bluntly, the false self is an illusion, and to allow our identity to be defined by and our behavior directed by the false self is madness. As individuals we have the power to act and change our experience of life whether anyone else does or not. "Because everyone is an individual and cannot wait until the collective unconscious of the whole race is cleared up," said Ernest Holmes, "everyone must break down the barriers which tie him to race belief. In so doing he will not only heal himself of the mesmeric effect of race thought, he will also be contributing to the final redemption of the whole race."[5]

Let's look at the underlying energy of the false self because we know that we are nothing but energy which is indestructible and neutral, that is to say, energy is neither good nor bad in and of itself. One label we give to that energy is love. Piero Ferrucci in his book *Inevitable Grace* notes that: "We all love someone or something—a person or an idea, power or pleasure, money or health, beauty or truth. ...Indeed, however limited this love, it contains a more or less hidden need for unity and happiness, and for this reason it must be taken seriously. We may call it *the principle of hidden longing.* ...a desperate longing for the eternal."[6] When the false self is in control, however, we are indeed looking for love in all the wrong places.

Now let's move on to look at the details of false self behavior, some of the specifics of the survival strategy. Thoreau realized that one goal of developing a "successful" survival strategy was to invent distractions in order to escape reality and to create the illusion that one could, in that way, avoid suffering. "He jealously guarded against what he perceived as the distractions of a 'normal life': 'Even the wisest and best are apt to use their lives as the occasion to do something else in

[life] than to live greatly.'"⁷   Thoreau was looking for simplicity, solitude and silence.

We can better understand the functioning of the false self if we break it down into its component parts, one being the security energy center. Western civilization has embraced the egocentric value of materialism (the belief that physical well-being and worldly possessions constitute the greatest good and highest value in life—*American Heritage Dictionary*). The almost religious devotion that western humanity has for rationality, efficiency and accumulation of material wealth has produced a human condition bordering on despair. Bordering on despair, my foot! Heck, it is despair! We must learn to call a spade a spade because denial is a fundamental behavior of the false self.

We will also come to understand the key role that fear has to play in each of the false self energy centers. In combination, the three energy centers of security, sensation and power keep us on the run with restlessness, anxiety, and an insatiable need for substances and processes to which we are addicted and which drive our worst neurotic behaviors. The despair is understandable but so is the way out of our dilemma.

The Security Center

The security center of the false self was described in a book entitled *Affluenza.* Columnist Maureen Dowd used this definition from the book. "...a painful, contagious, socially transmitted condition of overload, debt, anxiety and waste resulting from the dogged pursuit of more."⁸   The drive to constantly acquire more and more to feel safe never works and, on top of that, we are faced with constant anxiety caused by the fear of losing what we have managed to accumulate. We resemble nothing so much as anxious dung beetles scurrying about stacking up pointless piles of—dare I say it—crap!

The poet Kahlil Gibran poignantly describes the cost of this unconscious behavior.

> Verily the lust for comfort murders the passion of the soul, and then walks grinning in the funeral.
>
> For that which is boundless in you abides in the mansion of the sky, whose door is the morning mist, and whose windows are the songs and silences of night.
>
> Would that you could meet the sun and the wind with more of your skin and less of your raiment. [9]

The Sensation Center

> *I can resist anything but temptation.*
> Oscar Wilde

The sensation center is also called the affection and esteem energy center since we are constantly seeking love and also trying to find some way to increase our status or prestige in our community. What are the problems associated with these behaviors? There are too many for this short chapter but an important one was realized by early Greek philosophers.

> *Truth can only be seen if the philosopher detaches himself from pleasure.*
> Plato

Pleasurable sensations are ephemeral and often result in compulsive or addictive behaviors. They can then lead to boredom and the fear of a life without meaning, a life without anything to look forward to. Psychologist Philip Kavanaugh, in his book *Magnificent Addiction,* says: "We can become addicted to anything our mind can conceive....When we attempt to recover from unhealthy addictions and redirect this energy in more healthy ways we come up against major problems in this society: many addictions have become institutionalized, part of society itself."[10]   Anne Wilson Schaef also addressed this phenomenon in her book *When Society Becomes an Addict.* Our only hope, in the face of the reality of society as an addictive system, is to transcend society (P-B), choose a new narrative (P-A), a new identity, and stop our reactive behavior patterns.

To continue to choose to live with the old identity in the old story is an unfolding disaster well-known to most of us to some degree. Examples of the unsustainable future waiting for us are not hard to find. Jim Sullivan wrote in an article about the drug heroin: "Here's Steve Jones, Sex Pistols guitarist, about his long, slow dance with heroin after the Pistols fell apart, and he found himself penniless, at the end of the band's American tour in early 1978. 'The appeal for me is it totally made me not have to feel about anything, and that's what was great about it. It checks you out. It's not a social drug. I didn't have the suss [courage?] to go any other way, really.'"[11]   We must find that courage and then we will have the authentic power to heal our addictions.

The Power Center

> *Let me at least not die without a struggle, inglorious,*
> *but having done some big thing first,*
> *for men to come to know of.*
> >   Hector in the *Iliad*

The need for power and control in the human organism is a very strong and mostly unconscious drive. In his book *The Moral Animal Why We Are the Way We Are: The New Science of Evolutionary Psychology,* Robert Wright argues that: "We… have a relentless need for status and a propensity for doing almost anything to attain it….our genes 'know' even if we aren't always conscious of it, that higher status brings with it a better chance for survival."[12]   Wright has made the important point that the power, security and sensation centers are hardwired into our genes. The illusory pursuit of power and control is universal among human beings and a product of our need for survival in a sometimes ruthless and often indifferent society.

Constantly trying to control and manipulate events and other people causes conflict, jealousy, hostility and fear. Realizing at some level of consciousness that the power we covet offers no security, we fear facing up to that reality. The anxiety driven by our failure in turn leads to a compulsive seeking of that which we can never have, and we continue to chase the mirage of power in an endless nightmare in which ironically we have lost all power and control over our lives.

Philip Kavanaugh helps clarify the relationship between the need for control and the fear and anger which helps to explain the pervasive violence in American society. "Fear is usually the first symptom when control is threatened. Fear precedes anger, but the transition is so rapid that often we are not aware of the fear, just the anger."[13] Just as the crime of rape is about power not sex, violence is always about fear and power. Humanity is no stranger to power-driven violence even within the family as we all know. Will and Ariel Durant point out how common violence was in the family of 18th century Germany. "In the middle classes family life was subject to an almost fanatical discipline, fathers habitually whipped their daughters, sometimes their wives."[14] There is clearly a direct relationship between the pervasive fear in P-B, the belief that power and control is necessary, and the resultant psychopathology that seems to be on the increase in the global village.

Marcus Aurelius, as a successful Roman Emperor, had as much power and control as any person alive at that time and yet had no illusions about what that power meant. "Neither must we value the clapping of tongues, for the praise which comes from the many is a clapping of tongues. Suppose then that thou hast given up this worthless thing called fame."[15] Marcus Aurelius is right because in giving up power and fame we have lost nothing of value, we have lost nothing, because it never existed in the first place.

One of the most challenging aspects of the worldview underlying P-A is that of there being no "I." The foundation of the Buddhist worldview is *dukkha* (life is suffering), *annicca* (all form is impermanent and has no substantial reality), and *annatta* (the existence of a separate "I," "me," or "self," is an illusion). Grasping the illusory nature of a separate ego is for most of us more difficult than realizing the truths of suffering and impermanence. Psychologist Rollo May expresses the principle like this: "It is not unscientific sentimentality to point out, as Nietzsche and almost every other writer on ethics has done, that man in fulfilling himself goes through a process of 'transcending' himself."[16] To transcend the self is to lose nothing but rather to gain the only experience that is in fact "real."

"There's something …exhilarating about putting yourself on the side of *life*," said Joseph Campbell, "instead of on the side of protective *ideas*. When all of these protective ideas about life that you've been holding onto break down, you realize what a horrific thing it is, and you are *it*. This is the rapture of the Greek tragedy. This is what Aristotle called 'catharsis.' Catharsis is a ritual term, and it is elimination of the ego perspective: wiping out the ego-system, wiping out rational structuring. Smashing it, and letting life—*boom*—come through. The Dionysian thing smashes the whole business. And so you are purged of your ego judgment system by which you're living all the time."[17]

To do what Campbell suggests we must use the Point of Power Practice to stop reacting to the habitual influences of the false self. In the words of Ernest Holmes, "The mental patterns laid down in your subconscious throughout the ages can be consciously removed…There is no use wasting time speculating as to what avenue they came through. Your job is to reject them."[18]

We see people acting out roles they did not consciously choose, roles that offer no satisfaction, with identities and behaviors that bring them no authentic joy. Life is not theatre. We must abandon the contrived, fear-driven drama. We are caught up in a self-destructive role that is not natural for us—it is not our true self.

Our *job* is to choose the true self as our identity. As long as we accept fear-driven, false self attributes as our identity, we are alienated from our true self. Darkness and despair will be our future until we profoundly change, stop reacting to life and learn how to respond to the resplendent life we have been given.

Chapter Six

The Point Of Power Practice

Taking Complete Control Of Your Choices

We don't have to be highly intelligent to understand Simple Reality because it is indeed simple. We don't have to be highly disciplined spiritual ascetics, withdrawing from normal life to practice constant contemplation or meditation waiting decades for transcendence. Simple Reality is not complex or impossibly difficult and we experience the benefits immediately. The caveat here is that we do have to be awake, focused and motivated. Remember that we want our life to become an intentional meditation every moment of every day. The Point of Power Practice as the central focus of that meditation will provide us with the authentic power and positive use of energy to be successful.

> *He that is slow to anger is better than the mighty,*
> *and he that ruleth his spirit; than he that taketh a city.*
> Proverbs 16:32

The goal of the Point of Power Practice involves choosing to respond rather than react every moment of every day. Each time this is accomplished, we find ourselves experiencing Simple Reality. Because the goal of meditation when profoundly understood is seeing reality as it really is, we can say that in using this practice our life becomes a meditation.

When our past false self survival strategy or other conditioning is triggered, that moment is the point of power. At that "point" we are presented with an all-important choice. We enter P-B when we choose to react, to identify with the body, mind or emotions. What inevitably follows is the experience of afflictive emotions and suffering. If we pause, remain calm and breathe, choosing to respond, we will experience the "feeling" that characterizes P-A or Simple Reality. The breath is the "thread" that leads through the heart to the present moment and thus to the implicate order, which is the source of the wisdom and energy that connects all of creation.

To hear the same process described in a variety of ways might help internalize the meaning at a deeper level. For example, in choosing response over reaction one is able, as Marcus Aurelius said, "…to give the preference to the good thing…and freely choose the better, and hold to it."[1]

We can contrast the description above by a Roman Emperor/philosopher with the modern language of psychology. "The beginner learns to identify harmful behavior," says Daniel Brown, "and then 'practice the opposite' behavior… According to the laws of cause and effect such opponent action will manifest as positive changes in the stream of consciousness over time; behavior change contributes to intra-psychic change."[2] In other words we will have begun the process of shifting paradigms and acquiring a new identity. What follows is the new behavior of a compassionate, liberated person.

The whole strategy of the Point of Power Practice is to remain present while in the context of Simple Reality. Jane Roberts is referring to her book, *The Nature of Personal Reality* when she writes: "In this book Seth is saying that you can change your experience by altering your beliefs about yourself and physical existence…. Seth's main idea is that we create our personal reality through our conscious beliefs about ourselves, others, and the world. Following this is the concept that the 'point of power' is in the present, not in the past of this life or any other."[3] "You get what you concentrate upon."[4] The Point of Power Practice, choosing response over reaction, ensures that we are concentrating on a wholesome and sustainable narrative, something inherently "real."

Human suffering includes craving for plenty, pleasure and power. We all know the illusory nature of obtaining material wealth and feeling empty, of experiencing "pleasure" and still wanting more and having others within our "power and control" and still feeling helpless. The Point of Power Practice, choosing response over reaction, delivers authentic power, the power of choosing a sustainable story, a wholesome identity and compassionate behavior.

And finally to Ken Wilber who expresses himself in a fascinating, although somewhat, what can I say, "Wilberian" language. As a master synthesizer he is one of the few people who can give us both an eastern and western perspective. "For both Buddhist traditions the primordial state is one of immediacy. Events quickly settle before they become built up into constructs—time/space, self, gross percepts and thoughts....The meditator must learn to negate the more common forms of reactivity—expectations, doubts, evaluatory thought, and the incessant attempt to categorize the unfolding experience. Consciousness as we ordinarily know it in the West is not pure awareness but rather awareness as it is embodied in the psychological structure of the mind or the brain.... These two components, awareness and psychological structure, constitute a gestalt, an overall interacting, dynamic system that makes up consciousness. Techniques exist, however, that are intended to free a person's awareness from the dominance of the structure, of the machinery that has been programmed into him."[5]

Such a technique is the Point of Power Practice. Use it! You'll be glad you did.

Chapter Seven

Response And Reaction

Distinguishing Between Authentic And Illusory Power

In our world today we see all manner of human beings wielding power both with the sanction of society and outside the boundaries of the law. Our world is violent and dangerous. Many of our fellow humans are afraid, angry and suffering from all sorts of delusional behaviors. Within the minds of P-B inhabitants are beliefs, attitudes and values that are the source of the afflictive emotions that determine their reactive behavior. The great tragedy is that what they are reacting to or against has no substantial existence. What is the alternative?

> *Fear is excitement without the breath.*
> Fritz Perls

Let's begin with a look at what's involved with reaction. In psychological terms "reaction" is called physiological stress response (fight or flight). The reaction sequence is perception, then the psycho-chemical production of energy (potential afflictive emotion) and then the action taken, the *reaction*. The following example is of an unconscious collective reaction demonstrating the danger of living in P-B: the majority of heart attacks in the U.S. occur on Monday morning at 8:00 A.M. (This could be called an *aversive reaction*, caused by the dread of an imagined future experience.)

The sensation that triggers an initial reaction starts the first round of conditioned afflictive emotion, and then the second round of suffering comes with our chosen reaction whether it is identified with the mind, body, emotions or any combination of the three. That choice can be conscious or unconscious depending on how lacking in awareness we are of the nature of reality, that is to say, how much we are or are not grounded in the present moment. All triggers and reactions are a product of the human mind and are impermanent, hence illusory, or in other words, they lack substantial reality.

The conventional remedies recommended by therapists reveal a less than profound understanding of what is happening in a human reaction. For example a "fool your brain into thinking that you are in control" is a less powerful context than "you *are* in control" when you are triggered and the energy of the physiological stress response, the reaction, begins to occur. Indeed, we are all-powerful when we breathe and decide in that moment to respond rather than react. We have the choice to enter P-B, the realm of afflictive emotion and suffering, or P-A, the realm of the present moment where afflictive emotions cannot enter.

Psychologists could say that pausing to breathe and respond would be entering the beta state, named after the brain wave patterns associated with this type of response. I contend that although that happens, we need a much more profound context to reach the deepest "feeling" state of the present moment. Choosing the present moment is more than a physiological reaction; it is a response that takes us into a transcendent realm that with practice we can enter at will.

The following story is a classic illustration of the distinction between response and reaction. An older Samurai ready to retire to a life of contemplation and weary of the violence that too often characterized his life was ready for some peace. Although he had gained much experience in his conflict-filled life, only one thing remained a puzzle for him as he approached the end of his time on this earth. Sharing his question with a friend, he was directed to a monastic mountain retreat presided over by an aged and reputedly wise Zen master.

Shortly after arriving, following a long and arduous climb up the steep mountain, he was ushered into the tea room in which the sage with a long white beard sat on a cushion. The Samurai adjusted his two swords and lowered himself onto his cushion. After they had finished their tea the sage asked, "Why would a warrior want to travel so far to have tea with an old man not long for this world?" "I have come to ask a question of one reputed to be wise in the ways of this world and the next," replied the Samurai. "What is your question honorable Samurai?"

"I have only one concern that will disturb my days spent in meditation as I approach the end of my life and that is: What is the difference between hell and heaven?" With a slight sneer, the old man snarled and said, "Do you think a common, ignorant, simple minded oaf such as you could comprehend the answer to such a profound question?"

Astounded and furious, the Samurai leaped to his feet drawing his two-handed sword with one sweeping and violent arc. The sage raised his left hand and shouted, "That is hell!" The Samurai, caught off guard, took a deep breath and let the old man's reply penetrate to his heart. He smiled as he replaced his sword and slowly sank into his cushion. "And that is heaven," whispered the old sage.

> *But words are words; I never yet did hear,*
> *That the bruis'd heart was pierced through the ear.*
> Brabantio in Shakespeare's *Othello*

Ken Wilber quotes Heinz Hartmann, who seems to understand reaction and response, and can take us deeper into the psychology of reaction. "Evolution to Heinz Hartmann [the founder of psychoanalytic developmental psychology], is a process of progressive 'internalization,' for, in the development of the species, the organism achieves increased independence from its environment, the result of which is that...*reactions* [italics mine] which originally occurred in relation to the external world are increasingly displaced into the interior of the organism. The more independent the organism becomes, the greater its independence from the stimulation of the immediate environment."[1]

Understanding that we have a choice is critical to whether we can ever change our life's narrative and Deepak Chopra understood this. "In other words, most of us—even though we are infinite choice-makers—have become bundles of conditioned reflexes that are constantly being triggered by people and circumstances into predictable outcomes of behavior....Our reactions seem to be automatically triggered by people and circumstances, and we forget that these are still choices that we are making in every moment of our existence. We are simply making these choices unconsciously."[2]

Gandhi and Marcus Aurelius also understood what our objective should be in regard to reaction and response.

> *It is not that I am incapable of anger, for instance, but I succeed on almost all occasions to keep my feelings under control.*
> Gandhi

> *Let there be freedom from perturbations with respect to the things which come from the external cause...."*
> Marcus Aurelius [3]

Reaction is the false-self behavior in the illusory context of P-B. It is the false-self behavior, in effect, that created the toxic worldview (P-B). By resisting the temptation to act on our afflictive emotions we can move to response and compassion. We will be tempted continually by our conditioning and by the illusion of the pseudo-power we feel when reacting from the false-self energy center.

Here is a diagram of the sequence of being triggered, which always begins with fear, and then we either choose a response (creating compassion) or a reaction (creating suffering).

Response	Reaction
Fear (usually unconscious)	Fear (usually unconscious)
Afflictive emotions such as anger or jealousy	Afflictive emotions such as anger or jealousy
Pause, breathe and connect with reality *(The Point of Power Practice)*	Repress or act on the emotion
Response (creates compassion)	Reaction (creates suffering)

If we don't pause and respond consciously (The Point of Power Practice), we have lost the opportunity for choice. We are Pavlov's dog salivating and the steak is only an illusion.

> *I don't mind what's happening.*
> J. Krishnamurti

Krishnamurti lived most of his adult life in the narrative of Simple Reality and when asked to sum up his decades of teaching about the reality and power of P-A, he did so in the sentence quoted above. C. G. Jung would have agreed with Krishnamurti about the effectiveness of response over reaction. "The therapeutic measure of unresisting acceptance had proved its value yet again."[4]

We do have a choice to react or respond and the effects of that choice can even be measured physiologically. "For example, an MRI," reports Byron Belitsos, "can illustrate how the amygdala of depressed people behaves differently from non-depressed people. (The amygdala is a center of emotion in the brain, especially as related to memories.) When read a list of words that convey sadness, for example, the amygdala of depressives showed more than three times the duration of increased blood flow than those of their nondepressed counterparts. In other words, depressed folks ruminate [react] on sadness while well-adjusted others simply move on [respond]."[5]

Human intuitive self-understanding did not have to wait for modern science to point the way to Simple Reality. "It seems that long before modern brain research, the Buddha discovered [intuitively] how our minds are bound by instinct and habit [the false-self survival strategy], or—as he might have said—by both collective [the collective unconscious] and individual karma [reaction of the afflictive emotions]."[6]

> *Today I shall judge nothing that occurs.*
> A Course in Miracles

We (individually and collectively) create our own reality. Therefore, to create our reality and then go into afflictive reaction to that reality is an exercise in absurdity. Or as Deepak Chopra puts it: "Today I will accept people, situations, circumstances, and events as they occur. This means I will know that *this moment is as it should be,* because the whole universe is as it should be."[7]

"When you rail against an unfavorable environment, or a situation or condition… you are not acting independently, but almost blindly reacting. You are reacting to events that *seem* to happen to you, and always in reaction to a situation. To act in an independent manner, you must begin to initiate action that you want to occur physically by creating it in your own being."[8] This observation by our friend Seth calls for The Point of Power Practice which makes us the creator of our own experience rather than a reactor to what happens in the world of form.

Roman Emperor Marcus Aurelius no doubt had many opportunities to test his ability to respond to life. He seemed to have discovered his own Point of Power Practice. "For to be vexed at anything which happens is a separation of ourselves from nature…[and] the soul does violence to itself when it is overpowered [reacting] by pleasure or by pain.[9] "…leave these agitations [reactions] which are foreign to nature…"[10]

What are the rewards for those of us who make the commitment to choose response over reaction, to live our life as a Point of Power meditation? Is it worth the time and effort? Karen Armstrong seems to think so. "Living in this way, day by day, hour by hour, moment by moment, we would enjoy a constant, slow-burning ecstasy that leaves the self behind."[11]

Eckhart Tolle also is an advocate of shifting paradigms. "Whenever you accept what is, something deeper emerges than what is. So, you can be trapped in the most painful dilemma, external or internal, the most painful feelings or situations, and the moment you accept what is, you go beyond it, you transcend it….It may still be there, but suddenly you are at a deeper place where it doesn't matter anymore."[12]

I don't know about you, but what I have found is that choosing response instead of reaction, time and time again, is a life-transforming if not transcendent experience.

Chapter Eight

Intuition And Intellect

Choose Carefully Which Of These Human Attributes Is Charting The Course Of Your Life

As homo-sapiens we are justifiably grateful to possess the powers of human reason. We have used our intellect to move human civilization forward with a number of amazing achievements. But lest we be guilty of hubris, we should be mindful of the indisputable fact that we have yet to create a sustainable human community. Our relative progress won't ultimately matter if we fail to discover how we can harmoniously fit into the resplendently beautiful tapestry of Creation. The following observations will be helpful.

> *The heart has its reasons, which reason knows not of.*
> Blaise Pascal (1623-1662)

The following traditional story speaks to the distinction between intuition and the intellect. As God and Satan were walking down the street one day, God bent down and picked up something. He gazed at it as it glowed radiantly in his hand. Satan was curious and asked, "What's that?" "This," answered God, "is Truth." "Here," replied Satan as he reached for it, "Let me have that—I'll organize it for you." And thus began what we experience today as the human condition. Intuition, represented by God, has come to be been dominated by the intellect resulting in the human narrative we can call P-B. In P-A, the intellect (Satan) is subservient to intuition and regains his status as a "good angel" once again, no longer in rebellion.

The Greeks acknowledged two kinds of knowledge. First, the kinds of knowledge acquired with the categories of thinking found in Bloom's taxonomy with the three higher level thinking skills being analysis, synthesis and evaluation. The second type of knowledge is *gnosis* or intuitive knowledge. Gnosis means direct knowledge through sense experience, insights and knowingness.

> *But your ears thirst for the sound of your heart's knowledge.*
> Kahlil Gibran [1]

The head (intellect) has served us well in P-B, and can continue as the problem solver in the world of form. The intellect can invent machines, discover cures for disease, design buildings, and land humans on the moon, but the intellect is not capable of creating a sustainable future. Its proper role is subordinate to the heart, serving the higher aspirations of our inner wisdom. It is only through the heart (intuition) that we connect to our natural state of being, our true identity and to the perfection of Simple Reality.

Chapter Nine

Feeling And Emotion

Transcendent Joy Lifts Us Beyond The Suffering Of Afflictive Emotion

Speak what we feel, not what we ought to say.
Shakespeare—King Lear

Without a clear understanding of the distinction between feeling and emotion (as I define them) it is doubtful if humanity can learn to live on the planet in a sustainable way. I define feeling as our inner wisdom, our intuition; it transcends the intellect and our emotional reactions. Feeling is also what connects us to the implicate order, the source of the intelligence behind all of Creation. Feeling is what you know to be true whether you believe it or not. And as the poet Wallace Stevens reminds us, "The world about us would be desolate except for the world within us."[1]

Emotion, on the other hand, is a source of human suffering and has its origin in the illusion of P-B. I often call emotions "afflictive emotions" and Sakyong Mipham Rinpoche indicates why I might do this. "Being dragged around by emotions destabilizes our mind, our day, our life, and ultimately, the welfare of our planet."[2] "Our actual enemy, you see," says another Buddhist, Tenzin Gyatso, "is within ourselves. The afflicted emotions (pride, anger, jealousy) are our real enemies."[3] Even those emotions that we mischaracterize as "pleasurable" are correctly understood by many Buddhists as suffering. "*All emotions are painful.* This is something that only Buddhists would talk about. Many religions worship things like love with celebration and songs, Buddhists think, 'This is all suffering.'"[4] I think that Dzongsar

Khyentse Rinpoche is also correct in his understanding of the illusion of pleasure and the emotions associated with pleasure in P-B.

> *People say that what we're all seeking is a meaning of life. I don't think that's what we're really seeking. I think that what we're seeking is an experience of being alive...so that we actually **feel** the rapture of being alive.*
> Joseph Campbell (emphasis added)

I think that what Joseph Campbell is referring to is that life can only be "experienced" in the present moment. We will see in this chapter that many other very wise people have said the same thing. We find the same realization from both the Hindu perspective stated by Clive Johnson and the Buddhist articulated by Kay Mieno Kato. "Liberation does not come by merely saying the word 'Brahman.' Brahman must be actually experienced."[5] "To the Buddhist, the Truth is said to be inconceivable by the ordinary mind unless it could be experienced. Therefore, the possible best that could be done or presented by mere words could be such words as 'feeling Oneness.'"[6]

Speaking of Oneness as Kato has just done reminds us of our ability to respond to all of creation when we are in the present moment. Andrew Harvey urges us to keep that realization of Oneness in the forefront of our consciousness. "Let us go back to the source, and it indicates at once the Principle that bestows beauty on material things…. Our interpretation is that the Soul [true-self]—by the very truth of its nature, by its affiliation to the noblest Existents is the hierarchy of Being—when it sees anything of that kin, or any trace of that kinship, thrills with an immediate delight, takes its own to itself, and thus stirs anew to the sense of its nature and of all its affinity."[7] Harvey, of course, is speaking of what it "feels" like to be present in P-A. That affinity is our connection to all that is, our connection to the implicate order.

To experience "feeling" we must be in the present moment. To engage in the creative process is also a present moment experience. The word "inspiration" means "spirit within" and creativity is therefore an "inspirited process." It's easy to forget that the true-self is present throughout the human experience. Yes, even in the sometimes mundane institution of politics. Most of us are unaware of it most of the time. Sir Lewis Namier's Doctrine tells us that: "What matters most about political ideas are the underlying emotions [what I call feelings], the music to which ideas are a mere libretto, often of very inferior quality."[8]

If our political leaders would listen more to the melody of their feelings and less to the blaring cadence of power, they could learn to distinguish symptoms from problems. For example, they would not wage a "war on drugs" when the real problem is a people without a healthy identity, trying to anesthetize the emotions associated with the fear of being lost in a terrifying narrative with no effective coping skills, and alienated from the source of their power and strength, cut off from the ground of their being.

Afflictive energy flows from the energy centers of the false-self. It is important to remember that this energy shows up in the body, mind and emotions. Fear is the source of all afflictive emotions and drives the need for security, sensation and power. Fear energy is dark, ponderous and heavy. The energy of the present moment is light, buoyant and filled with joy.

Seth describes feelings eloquently: "Sometimes they rise to the surface, but in great long rhythms. You cannot call these negative or positive. They are instead tones of your being. They represent the most inner portion of your experience. This does not mean that they are hidden from you, or are meant to be. It simply means that they represent the core from which you form your experience.

"If you have become afraid of emotion or the expression of feeling, or if you have been taught that the inner self is no more than a repository of uncivilized impulses, then you may have the habit of denying this deep rhythm. You may try to operate as if it did not exist, or even try to refute it. But it represents your deepest, most creative impulses; to fight against it is like trying to swim upstream against a strong current....Once you learn to get the feeling of your own inner tone, then you are aware of its power, strength and durability, and you can to some extent ride with it into deeper realities of experience. It is the essence of yourself. Its sweeps are broad in range, however. It does not determine, for example, specific events. It paints the colors in the large 'landscape' of your experience. It is the *feeling* of yourself, inexhaustible."[9] (The italics are mine.)

Let's look at the relationship between the intellect or rational mind and feeling. "It [feeling] cannot be understood rationally," says Wayne Teasdale. "It is best approached through an *apophatic* method—a Greek term for a suprarational way of reflecting on the ultimate reality. It is a way of knowing God by *not* knowing."[10] It is a way of having the experience of P-A without letting the process of thinking become an obstacle. The British mystic Thomas Troward uses Christian mythology to support the importance of intuition, another word for feeling, over the intellect. "...the Creative Power is a process of *feeling* and not of reasoning....this is what is symbolically represented in the statement that God accepted Abel's offering and rejected Cain's. ... When a mere cold ratiocination is substituted for hearty warmth of volition, then Abel is symbolically slain by Cain."[11]

The irony in the following paragraph is that "thinking" strategies are being used to verify "feeling" wisdom. Feeling is beyond and superior to thinking and certainly beyond concepts, theories, models and indeed words themselves. "People studying neurocardiology, a new field," says Marc Barasch, "are discovering that the heart has a mind of its own. It has a brain-like grouping of neurons, and secretes oxytocin, the bonding chemical. Very often it seems there are certain perceptions that are first processed by the heart, not by the brain. So the knowledge that older cultures had—that the heart was at the center of the human being and not necessarily the brain—has some validity in science."[12] Mark Matousek, in his article in a highly unlikely source, the *AARP Journal,* also indicates that feeling and emotion have specific brain locations. "When you're really paying attention to the richness of the present moment, that's right-minded awareness. The left hemisphere is preoccupied with past and future."[13]

Continuing in this vein we have research cited in the annual report of the Institute of Noetic Sciences. "Turning our attention away from the brain, we focus on the heart. One of the quintessential scientific discoveries about the heart is that it plays a significant role in consciousness. At the Institute of HeartMath, scientists have established that the heart communicates with the brain and the body by way of both an extensive neural network and an electromagnetic field interaction. The electrical component of the heart's field, which permeates every cell in the body, is about 60 times greater in amplitude than the brain's. The heart's magnetic field is about 5,000 times stronger than the brain's and can be detected several feet away from the body with magnetometers. That gives the heart quite an edge on electromagnetic power.

"The heart's rhythmic field also has a powerful influence on processes throughout the body, and it appears to transmit physiological, psychological, and social information between individuals. In addition, research shows that the nervous system within the heart functions as its own "brain," enabling it to learn, remember, and make functional decisions independently of the brain's cerebral cortex. Experiments at HeartMath have demonstrated that the signals the heart continuously sends to the brain influence the higher brain centers involved in perception, cognition, and emotional processing."[14] Here we have the intellect supporting intuition which is the natural and healthier relationship between the two.

Psychology, of course, has something to say about feeling and emotion. The Greeks in their search for Simple Reality often spoke of the "good, the true and the beautiful." C. G. Jung thought deeply and also suffered excruciating pain in his search for an experience of reality. "A man cannot always think and feel the good, the true, and the beautiful, and in trying to keep up an ideal attitude everything that does not fit in with it is automatically repressed. If, as is nearly always the case in a differentiated person, one function, for instance thinking, is especially developed and dominates consciousness, then feeling is thrust into the background and largely falls into the unconscious."[15] Jung continues: "This interpretation emphasizes the belief that a patient must go beyond intellectual understanding and develop a feeling relationship with the contents of the unconscious."[16]

When we are not in the Now and are experiencing afflictive emotions, we are not psychologically healthy. "Depression and inflation are other names for mood," says Robert Johnson, "both give one a sense of being overwhelmed by something other than one's true self. This is weakness and incompetence in a man. Moods turn one to outer things or people for one's sense of value and meaning."[17] In other words, living one's life in P-B is a sure way to become and remain neurotic. A definition of neurosis: "Any of various functional disorders of the mind or emotions without obvious organic lesion or change and involving anxiety, phobias, or other abnormal behavior symptoms." Notice the key work "emotions" in this definition from *The American Heritage Dictionary*. Unfortunately, in the global village today neurotic behaviors are anything but abnormal.

In P-B we have two things upside-down. The intellect overrules intuition, and we have failed to understand that feeling, not emotion, links us to the profound guidance system of the implicate order in the context of P-A. "As a matter of psychological fact," Thomas Davis says, "mystical states of a well-pronounced and emphatic sort *are* usually authoritative over those who have them. They have been "there," and know. It is vain for rationalism to grumble about this....Our senses, namely, have assured us of certain states of fact; but mystical experiences [feelings] are as direct perceptions of fact for those who have them as any sensations ever were for us..."[18]

As we can now see, there is a direct relationship between truth and feeling. "Things are not true simply because someone somewhere first said them," writes Tom Harpur, "or because they are collected in books such as the Bible. They are true because they ring with full authenticity on the anvil of our souls."[19]

We must use P-B terms such as "soul" and "heart" judiciously, holding them "loosely" as it were, and then they can be useful. For example in the words of Sri Ramana Maharshi we can see that he uses the word "heart" as a synonym for our use of the word "feeling." "The seat of Realization is within and the seeker cannot find it as an object outside him. That seat is bliss and is the core [the ultimate depth] of all beings. Hence it is called the Heart....Entering the Heart means remaining without distractions. The Heart is the only Reality. The mind is only a transient phase. To remain as one's Self is to enter the Heart."[20]

One last distinction needs to be made and that is the one between compassion and sentimentality. Sentimentality and emotionality are closely related. Being sentimental means being colored by emotion rather than reason or realism. Sentimentality means being excessively or affectedly sentimental. Sentimentality is then, an afflictive emotion, it is a reaction driven by a false-self identity and as such is a source of human suffering. Any admiration of sentimentality is misplaced and reveals a lack of understanding of its true nature. Life in P-B, at times, all too sadly resembles a melodrama inhabited by whining victims who have chosen to deny their true identity and powerful ability to attain self-reliance.

In summary, speaking of power, we turn again to Thomas Troward who reminds us of our relationship to the source of all Creation. "…but as the individual's power of recognition expands, he finds a reciprocal expansion on the part of this intelligent power which gradually develops into the consciousness of intimate companionship between the individualized mind and the un-individualized source of it."[21] In the present moment, both the intellect and emotions are excluded as unnecessary remnants of the old story and all our questions simply fall away. "This is not the answer to our question [about feelings]," says Steven Harrison, "it is the question fallen silent…We are not the experiencers or explorers of this energy. We are this energy: expressing, exploring, manifesting, and disintegrating."[22]

In Simple Reality, we are neither seekers after truth, or manifestations of divine energy, we are the energy itself, perfect, inseparable and indestructible.

Chapter Ten

Paradigm B

The Emotional Reactions, Beliefs, Attitudes And Values Of This Age-Old Story Explain The Human Condition

History is a nightmare from which I am trying to awake.
        Stephan Dedalus in James Joyce's *Ulysses*

Paradigm B is the nightmare that we all live every day. It is the life that we have chosen albeit unconsciously by default and it is the experience of life that we have created. We are 100% responsible for that choice and our creation of it. We are also capable of making a different choice and have 100 % of the power necessary for creating a different reality. I know this is an "in your face" confrontation, but it happens to be the truth, as we shall see.

Peter Russell describes the "nightmare" mentioned above by James Joyce. "The realities of our day-to-day consciousness and of these moments of liberation are so difficult that it is almost as if a mental fence divided the two. On one side of the fence, I am caught in my mind—in my thoughts, my anxieties, my judgments, and my fears. I may on occasion recognize that this is all unnecessary, and that it removes me from the present moment, but such passing insights are seldom sufficient to release my mind from the grip of my conditioning. So deeply ingrained is my attachment to what I believe I should be thinking and doing, there seems no way over that fence. Indeed, for much of the time I have totally forgotten there is another way of being."[1]

How did we create P-B? P-B can be thought of as our "nemesis," the source of all of our suffering, of our self-destructive behavior. Clive Johnson speaks of our old friend the Goddess Nemesis in the guise of the sensation energy center—craving. "Desire arises from a sense of limitation and imperfection. A man of attainment [one living in the context of Simple Reality] feels no lack, what else is there for him to desire?"[2] And Seth further describes our tendency to "cling" to the very source of our suffering. "Many beliefs would automatically fall away quite harmlessly if you were being truly spontaneous. Instead you harbor them."[3] This is Seth's way of saying that we are shooting ourselves in the foot.

Paradigm B is focused on the illusion of form, both physical and mental. Jesus taught often about the pitfalls of allowing the false self to mesmerize us into thinking that the survival strategy was reality. "The Pharisees, with their appalling code of outward observances, were the only people towards whom he was really intolerant. A conscientious Pharisee of those days—and most of them were extremely conscientious, according to their lights—had an enormous number of outer details to attend to every day before he could feel that he had satisfied the requirements of God. A modern rabbi has estimated the number of such details at not less than six hundred…"[4]

P-B is a story in which the Oneness of Simple Reality has been shattered into pieces. This shattering includes alienating humanity from nature and people from one another. In his book *The Discovery of Being,* Rollo May observes that "Western man not only experiences an alienation from the human world about him but also suffers an inner, harrowing conviction of being estranged …in the natural world as well."[5] Authentic "being" or having an experience of P-A must involve feelings, beliefs, attitudes and values that support the reality of the wholeness, the inter-connection, the interdependence, the interrelatedness of all of creation. Otherwise we will continue to live with acute anxiety, an unnatural state for a human being.

> *When we remember we are all mad, the mysteries*
> *disappear and life stands explained.*
> Mark Twain

Mark Twain's observation seems to have been affirmed by Sigmund Freud when he chose *The Psychopathology of Everyday Life* as a title for one of his books. Jungian psychiatrist Laurens Van der Post joins in the observation of P-B: "…schizophrenia. It was so difficult to heal, I believe, because it was supported by a similar tendency to dichotomy in the spirit of an entire civilization backed up, as it were, by all that was negative in the 20th century *Zeitgeist,* and so it was in a sense incapable of cure without healing at the same time the mass of humanity and cultural pressures rallied unconsciously behind it."[6] Those "cultural pressures" have always existed in the fundamental nature of human consciousness and will remain until we choose to shift paradigms. In short, mental illness can never be cured in the context of P-B because P-B is the root cause of our self-destructive behavior and the neuroses growing out of it.

Everyone consciously or unconsciously behaves according to who they believe themselves to be (according to their identity), what they believe the nature of the universe to be (their worldview), and what they believe the nature of the Life Force which appears to be running things to be (Is the universe friendly or not?), and the relationship among all three. If our beliefs about these concepts are untrue (as in P-B), if they are outdated (e.g. some religious worldviews), or if they violate one's reason (e.g. Newtonian science), then our behavior will be self destructive. Bill Streett puts it this way in his article "Science and the Reenchantment of the Cosmos." "The vision of the mechanistic universe that grew out of Newtonian science fashioned social institutions that saw humans as efficient machines. In this fading worldview, a blind watchmaker created a clockwork universe without meaning or purpose."[7]

"The scientific creation story we've known, at its simplest," says Elisabet Sahtouris, "has come from physics and biology. Physics gave us a nonliving, accidental, purposeless, and meaningless universe, running down to its heat death by entropy, and biology doomed us to endless struggle in scarcity as nature's way of evolution—and thus our own human nature. This soulless materialist science scenario must be the most depressing creation story ever told. Yet our culture has created our reality from it, practicing scientific opposition to religion, believing we must get what we can while we can (usually at someone else's expense), building a now worldwide win/lose capitalist economy of cutthroat competition, and making material consumption the dominant lifestyle people have or aspire to have."[8]

Identifying with our intellect and surrendering to our survival strategy behaviors are only part of the problem here. Sahtouris continues: "After all, the foundational assumptions of science that nature is nonliving, nonconscious, nonintelligent, thus purposeless and meaningless, are unproveable beliefs stemming from a particular context of reaction against religion, prior to which all nature had been seen as alive."[9] We must not get from Sahtouris' description that religion is the answer because it is not. Remember that the institution of religion like all human institutions grew out of a P-B context.

There is no need for religion when we move beyond P-B because there is no spiritual journey, hence no need for a religious practice. There are no spiritual paths because there is no process. There is no goal because we are already at the point of choice which happens moment to moment each and every day. We do not need prayer or therapy because we are not dysfunctional or in need of healing or salvation. We are simply asleep, mesmerized and ignorant of the nature of reality. We only need to awaken. We only need to become present to Simple Reality.

Ken Wilber presses the attack on the intellect's tendency toward reductionism: "In these reductionistic accounts, rationality is the great and final omega point of individual and collective development, the high-water mark of all evolution. No deeper or wider or higher context is thought to exist. Thus life is to be lived either rationally, or neurotically (Freud's concept of neurosis is basically anything that derails the emergence of rational perception—true enough as far as it goes, which is just not all that far). Since no higher context [such as Simple Reality] is thought to be real, or to actually exist, then whenever any genuinely trans-rational occasion occurs, it is immediately explained as a *regression* to preoperational structures (since they are the only non-rational structures allowed, and thus the only ones to accept an explanatory hypothesis). The super-conscious is reduced to the subconscious, the transpersonal is collapsed to the pre-personal, the emergence of the higher is reinterpreted as an irruption from the lower. All breathe a sigh of relief, and the rational world space is not fundamentally shaken (by 'the black tide of the mud of occultism!' as Freud so quaintly explained to Jung)."[10] Whether we can grasp Wilber's amazing riff or not, we can guess that something in P-B is grievously amiss.

In contrast to Simple Reality (P-A), the Institute of Noetic Sciences describes the P-B worldview as including:

> Growth is good; more is better.
> Economic wealth is the truest sign of progress.
> "The market" is the most reliable measure of value.
> Individual selfishness serves the common good.
> We live in a world of scarcity.
> Humans are superior to other creatures.
> The Earth is ours to exploit.
> The world consists of "us" and "them."
> People are intrinsically bad.
> Technology—or God—will save us.[11]

How the initial stages of P-B developed are described by Ken Wilber. "…for the infant 'must gradually and painfully give up the delusion of his own grandeur.' Because there is now a separate self, there is now a separate other—the world is no longer its oyster. Researchers are fond of saying that at this stage, paradise has been lost …Because there are defects in self-structuralization at this primitive level of organization, the borderline does not have access to higher or neurotic defense mechanisms (repression, rationalization, displacement), but instead must rely on the primitive or less-than-neurotic defenses (particularly splitting, denial, introjection and projection)."[12] The challenge for us today is: how can we find our way back to our natural state of being after we have passed through the necessary developmental tasks of creating a relatively healthy but self-destructive ego? Not as difficult as you might think, but more about that in the chapter on Paradigm A.

*When we are born, we cry that we are come to
this great stage of fools.*
      Shakespeare, *King Lear,* Act IV, Scene VI

Paradigm B leaves us in an obdurate (hardhearted) state. We are hardened against "feeling" (compassion) which is the heart of P-A. All of our addictions whether substance related or process related are practiced to distract us, to moderate or repress the experience of suffering that characterizes P-B. Instead, we find ourselves in a state of continuous reaction, ironically increasing our suffering, or anesthetized and thereby deluded into thinking that we have found a sustainable coping strategy. We have fled more deeply into unconsciousness away from the very source of our salvation, the present moment. Thomas Moore said "a society that has lost its soul looks for security in the future and is willing to deny the reality of the present."[13]

The English composer Peter Warlock describes what it feels like to be lost in P-B. "I have been on a hopelessly wrong track for years, completely fuddled, *groping blindly in the dark* for something of whose very nature I was quite ignorant."[14] Seth suggests a way out: "If you dwell upon limitations, then you will meet them. You must create a new picture in your mind. It will differ from the picture your physical senses may show you at any given time, precisely in those areas where changes are required."[15]

Seth continues: "So you are locked into physical situations that are corroborated by the great evidence of sense data—and *of course it is convincing* because it reflects so beautifully, so creatively, and so actively, your own ideals and beliefs, whether they are positive or negative. In greater terms positive and negative have little meaning, for the physical experience is meant as a learning one. But if you are unhappy then the word negative has meaning…. Now let me give you a brief example of a core belief. It is a blanket belief. About it will spring events that only serve to reinforce it. Experiences—both personal and global—will come into the perception of a person who holds this belief, [and] that will only serve to deepen it further."[16] What Seth is saying is that P-B is self-perpetuating.

Let's look at the core beliefs that Seth is talking about on the collective level and their consequences with the example of the Israeli-Palestinian conflict. "Each side of the conflict, says Israeli psychiatrist Yitzak Mendelsohn, sees itself as a victim of history struggling to survive in a hostile world, with the other side as the ultimate threat to its existence. Individual biography is woven into a collective narrative of woundedness—what he calls a 'dependence on negative memory. People get hooked into a potent resentment that primes them for revenge and escalation [a classic reaction]. Hate becomes a way to create the illusion of power.' The task of reconciliation, he believes, is to break down the 'symbolic scars that bind people to the group' and offer 'some larger sense of "we" [a new identity in P-A] to replace the victim identity."[17] The victim identity is based on being caught up in the illusion of P-B but as *A Course in Miracles* reminds us, "These problems are not real, but that is meaningless to those who believe in them."[18]

The experience of Laurens Van der Post warns us of the folly of continuing to live in the madness of the old narrative. "History was written in a way that did not explain history and threw no light on its latent meaning. The legends and myths in which it has its roots and of which the dreaming process seemed so dynamic an element, as I had concluded in my amateur way. There seemed an underworld of history filled with forces far more powerful than the superficial ones that it professed to serve. Until this world was brought out into the light of day, recognized, and understood, I believed an amply discredited pattern of self-inflicted death and disaster would continue to reiterate itself and dominate the human scene."[19]

Two sad and disturbing metaphors can be used to describe the unconscious population of P-B. First, an unconscious person can be said to be asleep at the wheel. It's as if most of us begin our day staggering to the car in our pajamas and driving off down the freeway with a dream scenario playing in our fast asleep mind. This trip is bound to end badly and the numbers of fatalities and injuries will continue to grow on the streets and highways of P-B.

The other metaphor is suggested by the many "zombie" films created by filmmakers who were inspired consciously or unconsciously to address human unconsciousness and to depict the resulting disastrous consequences in a humorous way. The rapid growth of dementia also suggests a literal state of *non compos mentis* (not in control of the mind). This tragic "zombie-like behavior" is frightening and has profound economic and psychological implications for human communities.

> *Their destiny is destruction….*
> Philippians 3:19

Much of our survival strategy behavior is designed to cope with the horrors of living in P-B. Rollo May gives us an example from the myth of Oedipus used in the play by Sophocles. "When Oedipus learns the horrible truth that he has killed his father and married Jocasta, his mother, he put his eyes out. This is a very important act—'self-blinding' is literally what people do when they have profound inner conflicts. They blind themselves so that they are closed off…from the reality around them. Since Oedipus does this after learning how he has been living a delusion, we may take it as an act symbolizing the tragic difficulty, the 'finiteness' and 'blindness' of man in seeing the truth about himself and his origin…The drama gives us an age-old but ever new picture of the inner pain and conflict in finding out truths about ourselves."[20]   The truth will make us free if we can find the courage to confront our self-destructive story.

The creation of a survival strategy is natural and necessary and results in our creation of the context or story of P-B. When the initial stages of that process have been successful we have the choice of continuing to seek security, sensation and power or to respond to our natural inclination to experience the present moment. If our level of fear in P-B is too great, we may have repressed our true nature beyond the level of our awareness. In that case, we will not recognize that we have the choice of a new story and a new identity. We are then lost in the old narrative, which is the dominant condition of humanity today.

Taking the long view, humanity collectively and especially as individuals, can always awaken into the present moment and transcend the delusional paradigm. The Edgar Cayce readings, using the language of religion, are optimistic for the future of humanity in overcoming the influences of P-B. "For He will give thy efforts that necessary force, that necessary power, to quicken even those that are asleep in their own selfishness, in their own self-indulgences, and bring to their awakening that which will make for glorious activities in the earth."[21]

Saying the same thing as the Cayce readings in secular language, we can also support the cause of optimism for the future of humanity. A simple practice presents itself when shifting to present moment awareness (Simple Reality). This awareness is replete with authentic power and one is presented with choosing the power of self-reliance or the powerless condition of being caught up in the illusion of P-B.

It's at the "point of power" when our energy is activated by an environmental stimulus and we are faced with the opportunity to choose – choose to react and create afflictive energy by identifying with the body (a physical reaction), the mind (a mental reaction) or the emotions (an emotional reaction) – or choose to respond and thereby create compassion, freedom, joy and happiness by identifying with the wisdom of our intuitive true self and remain in the present moment. We have always had a choice to live in P-A and that choice is available to each and every human being on the planet each day.

Chapter Eleven

Paradigm A

By Embracing Our Authentic Power
We Can Create A New Sustainable Human Community

What are the characteristics of a healthy and life-sustaining story and, more importantly, are we capable of creating this new paradigm? Humanity's deepest thinkers have been asking that question since before Plato, and since Thomas More's *Utopia* (1516) gave that natural human yearning a name. Despite what the cynics may think, we are capable of choosing a different narrative and we have the power to bring it about. See what you think after reading this chapter.

This changeless Reality is pure consciousness...[1]

What if we were to synthesize all of the wisdom and effective transformational practices discovered by humanity thus far into one story (Simple Reality), a worldview of Oneness? Would the behavior of those who internalized this new narrative be affected? We have been unsuccessful so far in creating a sustainable culture. Some define culture as the totality of socially transmitted behavior patterns, arts, beliefs, institutions, and all other products of human work and thought characteristic of a community or population. I prefer the simpler definition of feelings, beliefs, attitudes and values. We have been unsuccessful in part because we have not been asking profound questions on how to create a sustainable human community let alone answering those questions.

How can we say that the Universe is friendly when there is so much "evidence" to the contrary? On the other hand, what if that "reality" is not what it seems to be? What if there is another way of looking at the evidence? What if there is a profoundly different perspective, a second reality not as apparent as the first? Many of the deepest thinkers who have lived on this planet say that this is the case. In this chapter we will meet some of those people and have the opportunity to examine what these divergent thinkers have said and then place it into the overall context of the new paradigm.

P-A cannot be described adequately in words or represented clearly by models or constructs, but can only be profoundly and completely embodied or "felt" in the present moment beyond all thinking. Nevertheless we can say that P-A is a state of realizing the inter-relationship, inter-dependence, and inter-being with all of Creation.

What does it "feel" like to live within the narrative of Simple Reality? In the words of Ken Wilber: "It [the true self] becomes a philosopher, a dreamer in the best sense; an internally reflexive mirror, awestruck at its own existence."[2] P-A is our awakened state or as Jung said, "He who looks outwardly dreams … but he who looks within awakes."[3]

Simple Reality includes a worldview, a story composed of our feelings, attitudes, beliefs and values. These are the aspects that our intellect can assist us with. John E. Mack describes it this way: "Worldviews, and the ways of knowing that produce and sustain them, structure our perceptions and define how we experience ourselves in relation to the universe. They determine how we relate to each other and to the Earth itself, how we find satisfaction, and how we come to terms with the ultimate questions of living and dying. For these reasons, there is no matter of greater significance than which worldview, or paradigm is ascendant in our society."[4]

It is helpful to make the distinctions between P-B and P-A in detail. The following partial list is meant to help us begin to get the feel of the profound difference between these two worldviews.

	Paradigm B (P-B)	**Paradigm A (P-A)**
Source of energy	Fear	Compassion
Motivation	Security, sensation and power	Feeling and compassion
Operational reality	Addictive system with co-dependent behaviors	Shared leadership in community
Relationships	Conditional love	Unconditional love
Operational dynamic	Competition	Cooperation
Dominant presence	False self	True self (Essence)
Ego states	Parent and/or child	Adult

Following are some of the feelings or emotions, beliefs, attitudes and values in P-B and P-A:

P-B	P-A
Secrets and denial	Honesty and truth-telling
Mistrust and entropy	Trust and truth-telling
Scarcity and problems	Creativity and abundance
Co-dependency and enabling	Self-reliance
Activities initiated by the leaders	Activities initiated by the people
Weak commitment to community	Strong commitment to community
Passive participation and exclusion	Decision by consensus
Problem avoidance	Working (solving) the problem
Fear, addiction, pain, sickness and sadness	Compassion, health, joy, peace, freedom and happiness

In addition to clarifying the differences between the two paradigms, we can also begin to entertain the possibility of a collective shift between paradigms, of moving humanity from one to the other. Donella Meadows in the following description emphasizes the importance of continuing to contrast the two paradigms, emphasizing the advantages of P-A over P-B. "How to Change Paradigms: 'You keep pointing at the anomalies and failures of the old paradigm, you keep speaking louder and with assurance from the new one, you insert people with the new paradigm in places of public visibility and power. You don't waste time with reactionaries; rather, you work with active change agents and with the vast middle ground of people who are open-minded.'"[5] The most effective and realistic paradigm shift, however, will involve one person at a time until a so-called "critical mass" is reached.

Psychology supports the importance of the worldview in achieving behavioral change. Daniel Brown confirms that: "Social psychologists have shown that alterations in one's outcome, expectations and belief system [worldview] have a significant impact on all types of behavioral change."[6]

In the context of Christianity we have Jung describing the implicate order expressing through each person. "The future indwelling of the Holy Ghost [implicate order] in man amounts to a continuing incarnation of God. Christ, as the begotten son of God and pre-existing mediator, is a first-born and a divine paradigm which will be followed by further incarnations of the Holy Ghost in the empirical man."[7]

The mystic, Thomas Troward, expresses P-A in still another way. "The spiritual kingdom is *within* us, and as we realize it *there* so it becomes to us a reality. It is the unvarying law of the subjective life that 'as a man thinketh in his heart so is he,' that is to say, his inward subjective states are the only true reality, and what we call external realities are only their objective correspondences."[8] The inescapable conclusion then is that the world of form has no substantial reality or meaning beyond that which we give it.

Mystics can be found in the most unlikely places but, of course, we are all mystics at heart. The following content relating to P-A was revealed by the mind of an academic, an intellectual and a professor of history – a very unlikely mystic. Joseph Campbell describes the insights of Professor Toynbee. "As Professor Arnold J. Toynbee indicates in his six-volume study of the laws of the rise and disintegration of civilizations, schism in the soul, schism in the body social, will not be resolved by any scheme of return to the good old days (archaism), or by programs guaranteed to render an ideal projected future (futurism), or even by the most realistic, hardheaded work to weld together again the deteriorating elements. Only birth can conquer death—the birth, not of the old thing again, but of something new.... Professor Toynbee uses the terms 'detachment' and 'transfiguration' to describe the crisis by which the higher spiritual dimension is attained that makes possible the resumption of the work of creation. The first step, detachment or withdrawal, consists in a radical transfer of emphasis from the external [P-B] to the internal world [P-A] …a retreat from the desperations of the waste land to the peace of the everlasting realm that is within."[9]

One of the most profound and deeply felt sources of the P-A experience is poetry. A poet often expresses profound feelings in the context of P-A. The best poets usher us into the realm of Simple Reality. Kahlil Gibran is such a poet.

Art
And if there come the singers and the dancers and the flute players, buy of their gifts also.
For they too are gatherers of fruit and frankincense,
and that which they bring, though fashioned of dreams,
is rainment and food for your soul [10]

Children
Your children are not your children.
They are the sons and daughters of Life's longing for itself.
They come through you but not from you.
You may give them your love but not your thoughts,
for they have their own thoughts.
You may house their bodies but not their souls,
for their souls dwell in the house of tomorrow,
which you cannot visit, not even in your dreams.
You may strive to be like them, but seek not to make them like you. [11]

Bernie Siegel reminds us of the importance of the relationship between our hearts and the narrative in which it is contained:

Our heart has something to say and we can do two things. Give it a nurturing story in which to say it and then speak. Your health and the future of humanity depend on it.[12]

We are very ambitious, we humans, but our ambition is focused on childish things. We do not aspire to serious pursuits; we find it difficult to put aside our fears and consider what is really happening around us. To do so will require that we transcend self-delusion, to admit that we have been clinging to beliefs that, when closely examined, do not make sense. How long have we been fleeing Simple Reality, how long have we persisted in our self-destructive behaviors and how long have we known that we have been doing this? For a very long time!

We close this chapter with one last look at the revelations left to us by the Eastern mystics found in the Hindu/Buddhist scriptures. Among the most toxic human beliefs driving many of our most self-destructive behaviors has to do with the illusion that we exist as separate individuals, as separate selves or egos. The American philosopher Emerson, after studying the *Upanishads* "would give perfect expression to the Hindu conviction that individuality is a delusion."[13]

> *They reckon ill who leave me out;*
> *When me they fly I am the wings;*
> *I am the doubter and the doubt,*
> *And I the hymn the Brahman sings.*
> From *Brahma* by Ralph Waldo Emerson

Historian Will Durant has a talent for paraphrasing the *Upanishads*. "The (non-individual) soul or force within us is identical with the impersonal Soul of the World."[14] The insight that *Atman*, the individual soul, and *Brahman* are one will be repeated by Jesus as 'The Father and I are one.' "The *Upanishads* burn this doctrine into the pupil's mind with untiring ... repetition."[15]

To lay aside the false self so addicted to the pursuit of pleasure, power and material possessions, and which lies at the heart of P-B, will require a story and a strategy little known in the West. The Judeo-Christian half of the globe "whose religion is as permeated with individualism as are his political and economic institutions" contrasts markedly with the "mystic and impersonal immortality—dominating

Hindu thought from Buddha to Gandhi, from Yajnavalkya to Tagore."[16]

Perhaps we should further qualify the source of our "ultimate truths" if we are going to dance with the mystics to the music of the ancient sacred insights. We will let Will Durant, and the brilliant philosopher Schopenhauer give testimony. "'In the whole world,' said Schopenhauer, 'there is no study so beneficial and so elevating as that of the *Upanishads*. It has been the solace of my life—it will be the solace of my death.' Here…are the oldest extant philosophy and psychology of our race; the surprisingly subtle and patient effort of man to understand the mind and the world, and their relation. The *Upanishads* are as old as Homer, and as modern as Kant."[17]

What is the strategy by which we can lay aside the craving and aversion of the false self and enter into *Nirvana* in which there is no individual consciousness? We must first consider the ultimate nature of our context: Where are we? Are we in a paradigm of many discrete parts, people separate from other people, people separate from nature, communities separate from other communities? Maybe a truer story is just the opposite. Maybe the narrative is characterized by the "good news" of Oneness in which all of the creation that we see around us is bound together, interrelated and mutually supportive when profoundly understood. Maybe what our deeper innate wisdom will tell us when we take time to listen is that we actually live immersed in the embrace of a natural, harmonious and peaceful narrative where we don't have to live in anxiety or compete with and destroy our neighbors and our environment.

"When we see ourselves as parts of a whole, when we reform ourselves and our desires in terms of the whole, then our personal disappointments and defeats, our varied suffering and inevitable death, no longer sadden us as bitterly as before; they are lost in the amplitude of infinity."[18]

We have looked at our first two "ultimate" realities, namely, no separate, isolated "me" and Oneness, rather than a "shattered" and threatening environment paralyzing us with fear. Next, we turn to the

Buddha and the First Noble Truth. In the Buddha we have the researcher who is without peer among the great teacher/mystics, using himself as his own lab rat. He sat in deep meditation and ran the maze of his own mind that revealed the most fundamental patterns of the human agony that most of us deny exists, even today 2,500 years later.

What we are loath to admit is that much of our survival strategy, which we use to distract ourselves from our existential suffering, is delusional. Our desperate seeking of power and control does not make us feel safer, our frantic accumulation of "stuff" does not deliver security, and the grasping of pleasures galore leaves us feeling that we are at the end of our rope. And indeed, we are at the end of the rope, choking for air. The very life-giving air that we seek is contained in our own breath which will lead us "within" and restore the ancient connection to the guidance system that will gently lead us out of our current dilemma. We know where we should go and how to get there, that knowledge is intuitive. The Buddha was not "special." He was in every respect just like you and me.

We must sever the illusory connection that we have to the body and its sensations, the machinations of the mind and our over-reactive afflictive emotions. Nothing so short-lived, nothing so ephemeral, should be taken as the substance of Simple Reality. The world of form, the sensations that exist "out there" reveal nothing about the world of Reality except what it is *not*. When we realize our human tendency to identify with our mind, body and emotions, we have discovered the origin of our dissatisfaction with life; we have revealed the causes of our personal suffering and the energy being used to create the unsustainable human condition.

Next, we humans pride ourselves on our capacity for reason. Durant continues his process of extracting the essence of the *Upanishad's* wisdom. "The first lesson that the sages of the *Upanishads* teach their selected pupils is the inadequacy of the intellect. How can this feeble brain that aches at a little calculus ever hope to understand the complex immensity of which it is so transitory a fragment? Not that the intellect is useless; it has its modest place, and serves us well when it deals with relations and things [P-B]; but how it falters before the eternal, the infinite, or the elementally real! In the presence of that silent reality which supports all appearances, and wells up in all consciousness, we need some other organ of perception and understanding than these senses and this reason."[19] What is this other organ of perception? "The highest understanding, as Spinoza was to say, is direct perception, immediate insight; it is, as Bergson would say, intuition, the inward seeing of the mind that has deliberately closed as far as it can the portals of external sense."[20]

The intellect in P-B is severely limited by the context of the story and engages in what Nobel Prize winner Sir John Eccles would call "premature cognitive commitments." Eccles is a neuro-physiologist who studies the mechanics of perception. He contends that, "...there are no colors in the real world, or smells, textures, or scents; they are structured in our awareness. Such perceptions are leading to the overthrow of the 'superstition of materialism' that the world is made up of matter and contains objects that are separated from each other in space and time. Everything is ultimately made up of atoms made up of particles moving at lightning speed around empty spaces. These particles are not material objects, but fluctuations in a field of energy. The cells communicate with each other through the language of neuropeptides, which are the biochemical equivalent of thought, he explains."[21]

It is in the process of meditation and becoming the observer of the illusion of the false self that we attain the insight of Oneness and experience the "feeling" of our connection with Simple Reality. Using the Point of Power Practice to enable us to choose response instead of reaction ushers us through the doorway into P-A. When we abandon the story dominated by the "head" and enter the narrative nurtured by the "heart" then we will find our way out of the maze that currently entraps us. Then we will experience the exhilaration of liberation, we will be free at last.

We were born with a longing for the joy, happiness, simplicity, peace, and compassion of P-A. But the immediate need to create a survival strategy takes precedence and we soon forget our true nature.

Returning to P-A is possible by giving a profound response to each of the three great questions:

Where Am I?
First we must remember where we are, and that question is answered in a single word "Oneness." We are contained in a paradigm where all of Creation is inter-dependent and inter-related, and therefore we *are* that Creation.

Who Am I?
We derive our identity from the answer to the first question. We are not separate from nature or each other, nor are we fragmented within ourselves with a separate ego, shadow, personal unconscious, or collective unconscious. We are an expression of pure, indestructible energy expressing beyond the illusion of time and space. Just as Creation is perfect and whole, so are we perfect and whole.

Why Am I Here?
We are here to experience reality. To do this and to avoid the pitfalls of the illusions of P-B, we must have an effective practice that keeps us in the present moment. In other words, the practice must empower us to respond to life rather than to react. Our conditioned, habitual reactions take us out of the present moment. The Point of Power Practice enables us to choose response over reaction, thereby experiencing the Simple Reality that is P-A.

Chapter Twelve

Paradigm Shift

*We Are All Born Into An Ongoing Story,
But We Don't Have To Remain There*

'Tis not too late to seek a newer world.
Tennyson

The power of P-B cannot be underestimated. It mesmerizes even those who might think that they have escaped its influence. Every existing institution and system of thought in the global village today had its origin in P-B and therefore perpetuates it. That's because every existing modern institution was only possible if it made sense within that narrative. If any theological ideas, scientific theories, philosophical concepts, theories of mathematics, etc. cannot fit into P-B they will be ignored, discarded or modified to conform to that paradigm. In other words, to be included in P-B, an idea must support it or it will not be accepted or indeed in most cases understood. To even think outside the dominant paradigm can be hazardous—think Socrates and Jesus.

Jesus' message was asking for a paradigm shift, a *metanoia,* a complete change in narrative. "The kingdom of God is at hand. *Meta noiete*: Change your Ways." (Mark 1:15).[1] The failure of Christianity to practice the teaching of its founder is precisely the failure to choose the identity that Jesus demonstrated.

To repeat, the problem we are going to have with changing our paradigm is that the old P-B narrative will not be able to accommodate that which is not included in the emotions, beliefs, attitudes and values of the old story. As Richard Edwards puts it: "The unorthodox is ignored because no one can believe it."[2]

Nevertheless, we can take comfort in the truth that, in a sense, P-B is a self-fulfilling prophecy, destined to self-destruct. As our experience in P-B becomes more and more irrational, we will perhaps find the motivation for change.

To escape the influence of P-B, characterized primarily by the illusion of duality, the conditioning of the false self, and the influence of the collective unconscious, we must begin with seeing clearly the distinction between P-B and P-A. The Buddhists call this "right view." Precepts such as the Ten Commandments or the Eight-fold Path are of little value since these are behavioral aspects of our identity and identity is driven by and defined by the context or narrative in which we are immersed. The "shift" must precede any identity change otherwise we are putting the cart before the horse and no authentic movement is possible.

Hence, P-B tends to maintain its dominance and has an enormous amount of inertia. For an individual to have an insight into another view of reality is not uncommon, but to shift paradigm, identity and behavior to a different worldview (P-A) is rare indeed. One barrier to a paradigm shift is that the paradoxes involved with P-A produce cognitive dissonance. For example, there is a process involved in shifting from P-B to P-A, and yet there is no process; it is difficult but easy; and intellectually the distinction between the two is, at one and the same time, difficult and simple.

The annual report by the American Psychological Association entitled "Stress in America," cites the other barriers to making "lasting lifestyle and behavior changes." They are lack of willpower, not enough time, and lack of confidence.[3] Other obstacles to the paradigm shift include: fear caused by the fundamental belief that the universe is not friendly which underlies the worldview of P-B; habit (conditioning) learned during the creation of the survival strategy of the false self; and unconsciousness (lack of awareness) caused by the avoidance of reality thought to be necessary to avoid pain and suffering.

Seth offers hope in the possibility of change. "You can stub your toe as easily on a misplaced idea as you can upon an old chair. It will help you, in fact, if you think of your own beliefs as furniture that can be rearranged, changed, renewed, completely discarded or replaced. Your ideas are yours. They should not control you. It is up to you to accept those that you choose to accept…In order to dislodge unsuitable beliefs and establish new ones, you must learn to use your imagination to move concepts in and out of your mind. The proper use of imagination can then propel ideas in the direction you desire."[4] Moving concepts in and out of our mind is one of the goals of this chapter—but only a preliminary one.

A paradigm shift does not depend, as Seth has indicated, on any changes outside of oneself. We can all successfully learn to live in the present moment by making our life a meditation on Simple Reality. In all of the "Seth books" by Jane Roberts the following statement is found at the heart of Seth's teaching. "I cannot say this often enough: Your beliefs form your reality, your body and its condition, your personal relationships, your environment, and *en masse* your civilization and world."[5] Beliefs are vitally important but they form only one of the components of worldview— defined as beliefs, attitudes, values and emotional reactions.

The behavior involved for an individual to bring about a paradigm shift is relatively easy to understand, but collective paradigm shifts, often related to evolution and to the theory of "critical mass" energies, are more difficult to support. The idea of a collective paradigm shift, however, is not new. "In the wake of the Newtonian revolution, Johann Wolfgang von Goethe (1749-1832) dared to propose a different sort of science that was …holistic, participatory, and qualitative….Through painstaking research, he established a three-step method of investigation designed to facilitate the perception of phenomena directly."

David Feinstein continues his explanation of Goethe's theory in his article entitled "Subtle Energy: Psychology's Missing Link": "The first step is to change one's mode of consciousness to the intuitive-holistic mind, commonly found in indigenous worldviews, through such practices as drumming, ecstatic dance, or a general change in attitude toward one of thanksgiving, respect, and receptivity. The next step, active observation, rests on the belief that the observer affects the observed, an idea that is integral to quantum theory, which came nearly a century after Goethe. The last step of Goethe's method asks the researcher to become an organ of expression of the phenomenon, like the shaman who becomes possessed by a plant, animal, or nature spirit in order to gain knowledge or power and then communicate from that perspective."[6] The modern and pragmatic equivalent of the practices mentioned above is the Point of Power Practice, so simple and yet more effective.

Paradigm shifts can be found throughout human history. When did the "minor shifts" in awareness, as opposed to the shift of Self-realization, occur? (Not all such shifts, by the way, have been positive.) One such shift, one of the most recent, was the shift from intuition to greater emphasis on thinking or dependence on the intellect. Christopher Porterfield gives us an example of how it manifested in the realm of classical music. "Bach was the father of the Baroque, the waning age of myth and mysticism [feeling]; Frederick [the Great of Prussia] was a son of the Enlightenment, the dawning epoch of empiricism and reason [thinking]. Their musical duel took place at the 'tipping' point between ancient and modern cultures….the moment at which 'the intuitions, attitudes and ideas of a thousand years were being exchanged for principles and habits of thought that are still evolving and in question three centuries later."[7] In this example, Frederick challenges Bach's outmoded music as well as his prowess on the keyboard, thinking that he could show up the older man. Big mistake! Oh well, that's what the intellect-driven ego does, especially a large ego.

Many great minds from different disciplines and backgrounds have conceived of a collective paradigm shift. Psychologist, Robert Johnson, found this very interesting but I don't think we should be surprised. "It is fascinating to me that three great figures of the twentieth century occupying almost exactly the same lifespan—Carl Jung, the scientist; Teilhard de Chardin, a Catholic theologian; and Sri Aurobindo, a Hindu mystic—each talked of the new consciousness and new world order, though each spoke in the language of his own discipline."[8]

Ever the optimist, Willis Harman, was a lifelong promoter of the collective human potential to shift paradigm. "We are living through one of the most fundamental shifts in history—a change in the actual belief structure of Western society. No economic, political, or military power can compare with the power of a change of mind. By deliberately changing their images of reality, people can and are changing the world."[9] I am afraid that any lasting change will take more than modifying the images of reality.

Jung found that a profound change in the human narrative also shows up in our dreams. "He [Jung] saw that the number three represented a consciousness that was time-dominated, devoting to acting, doing, processing, accomplishing. We live in an age that holds a Trinitarian view of theology. The doctrine of the Holy Trinity is basic to the Christianity of our time, and the Holy Trinity is an exact model of our modern consciousness. The number four, though, denotes being, eternity, peace, and contemplation....Often the dreams directly involve three turning into four..."[10]

Do we have a choice with respect to shifting the human worldview? Rollo May thinks the challenge is daunting but describes impressive rewards. "We are called upon to do something new, to confront a no man's land, to push into a forest where there are no well-worn paths and from which no one has returned to guide us. This is what the existentialists call the anxiety of nothingness. To live in the future means to leap into the unknown, and this requires a degree of courage for which there is no immediate precedent and which few people realize.... Whereas moral courage is the righting of wrongs, creative courage is the discovering of new forms, new symbols, new patterns on which a new society can be built.... My point is that creativity of the spirit does and must threaten the structure and presuppositions of our rational, orderly society and way of life.... Plato in his beautiful dialogue the *Symposium*, described what he called the true artists—namely, those who give birth to some new reality. As I would put it, these are the ones who enlarge human consciousness. Their creativity is the most basic manifestation of a man or woman fulfilling his or her own being in the world."[11]

> *We cannot solve our problems at the same level* [or within the same paradigm] *of consciousness with which we created them.*
> Albert Einstein

Now we get to the challenging aspect of the paradigm shift, how to do it. We already know the essence of the process embodied in the Point of Power Practice and simply moment by moment, day by day choosing response over reaction. In addition, in my own experience, I supported my paradigm shift by becoming less focused on the outer and more focused on my inner world. That involved simplification including less dependence on technology. I was fortunate in that I could get by with basic phone service, no internet, and no cell phone. I was able to protect my solitude by maintaining an environment that was conducive to contemplation 24-7. This is the ideal, but for most not practical. The absence of the ideal (simplicity, solitude and silence) is not a barrier to the paradigm shift. The Point of Power Practice is sufficient to shift paradigm, to transform our attitudes, beliefs, values and emotional reactions.

The failure to attain Simple Reality, which begins with the shift from P-B to P-A, can be a failure to have the "insight" or to attain the realization of Oneness. Life in a P-B context or story tends to mesmerize human beings with the ego or false self as the center of a pseudo-reality. In that state we lurch about in a zombie-like quest for meaning with no hope of attaining satisfaction until we escape the narrative that enthralls us—until we shift to the worldview of Oneness—P-A.

In the book *The Power of Myth,* Bill Moyers asks Joseph Campbell how human consciousness is transformed or in other words how can we shift from P-B to P-A. Campbell answers: "Either by the trials themselves [suffering] or by illuminating revelations [insights]. Trials and revelations is what it's all about."[12] Trials are common enough. We face the continuous day-to-day, moment-to-moment challenge of our past conditioning and the habit of reacting to the unavoidable reality of life on this planet. That is life in P-B. Revelations are equally available. We have only to look within to our profound and natural state of being which will reveal the truth and beauty of the life we have been given. Then we will have become the change we are seeking.

The mystic Thomas Troward had a lot to say about the paradigm shift. "…the basis of all healing is a change in belief. …therefore, what relatively to man, we call his creative power, is that receptive attitude of expectancy which, so to say, makes a mold into which the plastic and as yet undifferentiated substance can flow and take the desired form…. First, the whole train of causation is started by some emotion which gives rise to a desire; next the judgment determines whether we shall externalize this desire or not; then the desire having been approved by the judgment, the will comes forward and directs the imagination to form the necessary spiritual prototype; and the imagination thus centered on a particular object creates the spiritual nucleus, which in its turn acts as a center round which the forces of attraction begin to work, and continue to operate until, by the law of growth, the concrete result becomes perceptible to our external senses."[13]

Troward was one of the most profound theorists for New Thought which teaches, rather than being a victim of the mind, the mind could be used as a medium for creating whatever one could embody in consciousness. The caution here is "be careful what you ask for." If we ask for the experience of Simple Reality while in the context of P-A, we can't go wrong. What we are doing is making our life a meditation, continually choosing response over reaction, in order to have that experience of Simple Reality.

From the pages of the magazine *Shift: At the Frontiers of Consciousness:* "Matter and spirit are meeting. Thoughts transform into physical reality. We see what we want to see. We see what we create. We are what we think. This growing consciousness changes politics, economics, science, and the arts. Scientific discoveries and spiritual growth lead to a new paradigm, just as it did when

Copernicus postulated the Earth revolved around the Sun or when Newton calculated gravity."[14]

Let us take encouragement from the insightful words of Ken Wilber. "At every stage of development, the next higher stage always appears to be a completely 'other world,' an 'invisible world'—it has literally no existence for the individual, even though the individual is in fact *saturated* with a reality that contains the 'other' world. The individual's 'this-worldly' existence simply cannot comprehend the 'other-worldly' characteristics lying all around it."[15] That is why an immersion in this material is so important and the meditation and Point of Power Practice are so effective. In so doing we are peeling away the layers of the "this-worldly" existence.

Wilber continues, "In other words, the real problem is *not* exterior. The real problem is *interior*. The real problem is how to get people to *internally transform* from egocentric to sociocentric to worldcentric consciousness, which is the *only* stance that *can* grasp the global dimensions of the problem in the first place, and thus the *only* stance that can freely, even eagerly, embrace global solutions. ...In other words, global consciousness is not an *objective belief* that can be *taught* to anybody and everybody, but a *subjective transformation* in the interior structures that *can* hold the belief in the first place..."[16] Simple Reality contains those "interior structures" that support the paradigm shift.

The IONS annual report for 2008 emphasizes the importance of distinguishing between P-B and P-A. "As we explore ways in which a new story about our lives and the universe can emerge, it might be useful to draw an analogy to a form of psychological healing known as 'narrative therapy.' When people seek help from a therapist, they arrive with a story that explains their difficulty. Narrative therapists inquire into this 'problem story' to seek out those details that their client has overlooked—details that tell a different story, that can rewrite the problem narrative. The focus is redirected to the intentions, dreams, values, and events that speak of forgotten competence and heroism. In a similar way, we can redirect our focus to innate human qualities such as compassion and generosity that we must cultivate in order to fully participate in the evolutionary forces of our time."[17]

Emerson makes that all-important distinction between truth and illusion as only he can. "Men, such as they are, very naturally seek money or power; and power because it is as good as money—the 'spoils,' so called, 'of office.' And why not? For they aspire to the highest, and this, in their sleep-walking, they dream is highest. Wake them and they shall quit the false good and leap to the true, and leave government to clerks and desks."[18]

In a book written over a half century ago, Rollo May illustrates the futility of trying to understand human self-destructive behavior from within the context of P-B. He analyzes American behavior in the middle of the twentieth century and arrives at conclusions that appear plausible but focused on symptoms rather than the underlying causes that are revealed in P-A.

"…everyone would agree that in times of social upheaval, like our own, [the Depression, the Cold War, McCarthyism and the threat of the A-bomb] people suffer from feelings of 'rootlessness' and tend to cling to authority and established institutions as a source of security in the storm. As Dr. and Mrs. Lynd point out in their study of the American town during the depression, in *Middletown in Transition,* 'Most people are incapable of tolerating change and uncertainty in all sectors of life at once.' So the citizens of Middletown were turning toward more conservative authoritarian beliefs in economics and politics, more rigid moral attitudes, and were joining in increased numbers the conservative, fundamentalistic rather than the liberal churches."[19]

What should be seen by all observers of human behavior, whether today or any time in the past, is the self-destructive expression of the energy centers of the false self which is controlling the narrative, the identity and hence the behavior of virtually all of humanity. May makes an important conclusion related to the importance of the human context, the limiting effect of P-B. "But no 'ego' moves on into responsible selfhood if it remains chiefly the reflection of the social context around it."[20]

"The traditions are in agreement that enlightenment produces two major changes: the view of external reality is permanently altered and the internal experience of suffering is alleviated. Both changes are derived from the shift in the association between awareness and mental events that occurs during enlightenment."[21] Here Ken Wilber has revealed the substantial rewards for engaging in the process of leaving P-B and entering Simple Reality

Moving on to the context of religion we learn an important aspect of the paradigm shift from Naropa who was one of the early teachers of Buddhism. Chogyam Trungpa Rinpoche describes how sudden the insight can be. "That was quite interesting and shocking. Naropa achieved realization in a sudden glimpse….He experienced life as a mirage….Then there is transference of consciousness. Since you do not believe in physical existence as a solid thing that you can take refuge in, you can switch out of such a belief into non-belief, transfer your consciousness into open space, a space which has nothing to do with the fixed notion of 'me and mine' and 'that and this' at all….The whole thing is seen as open, brilliant, as things as they really are. There are no mysterious corners left."[22]

Most people contained in a religious narrative cannot see Simple Reality even though it is found in all major religions. For example, the concept often found in various theologies referring to being "born again" is the usually imperfect understanding of the necessity of a paradigm shift. For example, in Christianity we find in the New Testament (John 3:6-14): "That which is born of the flesh is flesh. That which is born of the Spirit is spirit. Do not marvel that I said to you, 'You must be born anew.'" Being "born of the Spirit" is simply to enter the Now. The Now is our natural state of consciousness but is "overridden" by our false-self behaviors.

Beginning with Adam we see resistance to living life in the present moment. "The anxiety in Adam," observes Rollo May, "and the torture experienced by Prometheus also tell us psychologically that within the creative person himself there is fear of moving ahead. In these myths there speaks not only the courageous side of man, but the servile side which would prefer comfort to freedom, security to one's own growth."[23] "Thomas Merton suggests that there is an existential anxiety crisis that precedes the final integration of life as a 'new man.' He tells us that this anxiety is a necessary partner to psychic rebirth, the birth of the person into a higher level of functioning and perceiving and feeling."[24]

> *Therefore if any be in Christ, he is a new creature; old things are passed away; behold all things are become new.*
> Psalm 103:12

Jesus in *A Course in Miracles* speaks specifically of the paradigm shift. "God's Will is all there is. We can but go from nothingness to everything; from hell to Heaven. Is this a journey? No, not in truth, for truth goes nowhere. But illusions shift from place to place; from time to time. The final step is also but a shift. As a perception it is part unreal. And yet this part will vanish. What remains is peace eternal and the Will of God."[25] Joseph Campbell describes the shift mentioned by Jesus in this way: "The New Testament teaches dying to one's self, literally suffering the pain of death to the world and its values [P-B]."[26]

The resurrection of Jesus is a metaphor for the shift from P-B to P-A as Thomas Aquinas writing in *Summa Theologiae* came close to understanding. "In rising, Christ did not come back to life in the usual sense of life as we all know it; rather, he entered a life that was somehow immortal and godlike."[27] In the narrative of P-A we understand that we are immortal energy, not subject to an identity based on the body, mind or our emotional reactions. We began our human journey at a fork in the road, not in a garden with a serpent. We create horrific suffering and an unsustainable future if we continue each day to choose the road that leads to P-B. If we choose P-A, we create a sustainable community in harmony with all of creation and a life lived in the present moment filled with compassion.

John Van Auken found in the New Testament book of John that: "... Jesus is talking to Nicodemus and refers to that natural state [the Now] telling Nicodemus that he will not ascend to heaven but that he is already in heaven. Later in the book of John he is talking to Thomas and Philip and says when asked about the Father, 'Don't you believe that I am in the Father, and the Father is in me?' (John 14:4-11)"[28] Oneness is the P-A principle being referred to here, meaning that there is no duality. We are one with P-A and it is our natural state which we cannot separate from except in the delusion of P-B, and that separation exists only in our mind. So the paradigm shift is only a *recognition* of already being contained in P-A, with the natural identity that such realization implies.

Again, Jesus in *A Course in Miracles:* "What the world is, is but a fact. You cannot choose what this should be. But you can see how you would see it. Indeed, you *must* choose this."[29] Heaven (P-A) is here and now and the Father and I are one. Creation is perfect and we are all a perfect part of that creation. We have only to realize in a paradigm shift that perfection which always was and always will be. It is not too late to "choose" that realization.

Chapter Thirteen

Meditation

Practicing Meditation, We Can Reveal Our True Identity And Profoundly Enhance Our Experience Of Life

All man's miseries derive from not being able to sit quietly in a room alone.
Blaise Pascal

In the context of Simple Reality the purpose of meditation is to attain an experience of the present moment. In pragmatic language the purpose of meditation is to enable the choice of response rather than reaction. Obviously then, a profound practice of meditation means that our life becomes a continuous meditation employing the Point of Power Practice. It then is a simple matter to assess how successful we are from moment to moment at living in P-A as opposed to P-B. Am I at this moment experiencing the afflictive emotions of a reaction or the "feeling" of the Now? The following material on meditation will support the simple Point of Power Practice.

The reason that we must not identify with the mind, body and emotions, for example, is because it is through them that we express fear and this expression is the reaction that is the root cause of human suffering. It is through the practice of meditation that we begin developing the awareness that will allow our new identity to emerge.

Meditation for the beginner has a very specific goal. Focusing on the breath and observing the body, mind and emotions will begin to reveal the reality of impermanence. Sensations in the body come and go. The story (P-B) contained in the "monkey mind" shifts and changes in an endless stream of consciousness. The story also drives emotional reactions that feed energy back into the story and the emotions also morph endlessly into never-ending sources of suffering.

By focusing on and returning our attention to the breath, as we also continue to observe the body, mind and emotions, we will eventually experience a sense of separation between that which is being observed and our true self as the observer or witness. The realization that we are the observer and *not* our body, mind or emotions shifts our identity and we experience the insight which becomes the foundation for the actual shift into the present moment. Focusing on the breath can also transform energy from a reaction into a response. When this occurs we have had the experience of moving from P-B to P-A—we have had an experience of Simple Reality. By focusing on the "grounding" influence of the breath and choosing response over reaction—we have chosen feeling instead of afflictive emotion.

Our life then becomes a meditation in the context of P-A wherein we get more and more secure in our identity as pure indestructible energy in the narrative of Simple Reality or Oneness. We are aware that we are engaged in the moment to moment process of reconditioning our behavior. We have had decades of training to react to the fear-driven craving and aversion associated with the three energy centers of the false self. Like the dog in Pavlov's conditioning experiments, we automatically salivate when we hear the bell, the ringing desire for security, sensation and power that trigger our reaction. Because we have a new identity and the Point of Power Practice to employ in a constant state of vigilant meditation (present moment awareness), we are empowered to choose to not salivate (react) but instead we choose to remain in the Now and respond with our new identity. We are attaining freedom from the effects of the bell, freedom from the self-destructive influence of P-B. Meditation and life have merged in a compassionate, joy-filled dance to the music of the Universe.

Now, taking a broader look at meditation as defined and practiced by wise and perceptive teachers who lived across the space/time continuum of human history, we find a meditation technique that was faithfully preserved and passed down in a direct lineage from the Buddha. The ancient Indian meditation technique called *Vipassana* was rediscovered 2500 years ago by Siddhartha Gotama (Buddha). The term Vi*passana,* translated as "Insight" meditation by some, means "seeing things as they really are" or for our purposes it means Simple Reality.

Using the process of observing the breath we learn that we are not our body, mind or emotions. The Buddhists who practice *Vipassana* would say that they are realizing the universal truths of impermanence, suffering and egolessness or purification of the mind by self-observation. This is true and I would say, more simply, that we become the observer of our own false self, transcend P-B illusions, and enter the present moment (P-A) feeling the freedom, peace, compassion, joy and happiness of Simple Reality, reality as it really is. In so doing our identity shifts because we have provided a new worldview or context that will accommodate it.

The following story from Henepola Gunaratana shows the functioning of the mind and breath in the contexts of both P-B and P-A. "Ancient Pali texts [the *lingua-franca* spoken during the life of Siddhartha Gotama] liken meditation to the process of taming a wild elephant. The procedure in those days was to tie a newly captured animal to a post with a good strong rope. When you do this, the elephant [the mind identified with the body, the P-B story and the emotions] is not happy. He screams and tramples, and pulls against the rope for days. Finally it sinks through his skull that he can't get away, and he settles down. At this point you can begin to feed him and to handle him with some measure of safety. Eventually you can dispense with the rope and post altogether, and train your elephant for various tasks. …In this analogy the wild elephant is your wildly active mind, the rope is mindfulness [meditation or Point of Power Practice], and the post is our object of meditation, our breathing [our ability to respond]."[1] A mind in P-A is a tamed mind, a disciplined mind that can distinguish between reaction and response and is willing to work day in and day out to attain true freedom.

Simple Reality and the three basic causes of suffering (craving, aversion and ignorance) are mutually exclusive. The meditation practice of continually choosing response and not reacting is a process of reconditioning our behaviors or "purification" as the Buddhists would say. In short, this practice of meditation when combined with the Point of Power Practice eliminates all of our suffering caused by our reactions, because we simply are empowered to choose response instead of reaction. We have developed a new identity, characterized by self-reliance and the authentic power to transcend the unconscious narrative and the delusional identity of P-B. It no longer makes sense to choose self-destructive and reactive behavior, so we stop doing it.

Why the Point of Power Practice as opposed to other forms of meditation and why must our day-to-day life become a meditation? S. N. Goenka has taught *Vipassana* meditation for over 40 years. He says, "There are many techniques to develop concentration. One may be taught to concentrate on a word by repeating it, or on a visual image, or even to perform over and over again a certain physical action. In doing so one becomes absorbed in the object of attention, and attains a blissful state of trance. Although such a state is no doubt very pleasant so long as it lasts, when it ends one finds oneself back in ordinary life with the same problems as before. These techniques work by developing a layer of peace and joy at the surface of the mind, but in the depths the conditioning remains untouched. The objects used to attain concentration in such techniques have no connection with the moment-to-moment reality of oneself."[2] That "moment-to-moment reality" which must be dealt with is the continuous reaction emanating from our P-B conditioning.

How powerful is the Point of Power Practice? It is based on the meditation practice taught by the Buddha himself and reaffirmed by S. N. Goenka, who has become a world-renown teacher of *Vipassana* meditation. "One doesn't react, and not reacting starts changing the habit patterns at the deep level of the mind....In my experience, I haven't found a single person who has been unable to do it....Unless there is peace in the mind of the individual, how can there be peace in the world?"[3]

In addition to the Simple Reality principles of impermanence and suffering, perhaps the most difficult to internalize is that of no "self" or no "I." It takes a healthy ego or personality to contemplate the reality of not having an existence separate from the rest of creation. But Jack Engler warns of the dangers of insisting on "self-centeredness." "You have to be somebody before you can be nobody. This is the paradox relating to the Buddha's teaching relating to 'no self.' On the other hand, my experience teaching Buddhist psychology and *Vipassana* meditation has made it equally clear that clinging to a sense of personal continuity and self-identity results in chronic discontent and psychic conflict…."[4]

> *Enlightenment is an accident: meditation makes you accident prone.*
> Richard Baker Roshi

What are the fruits of a regular meditation practice that we haven't mentioned specifically? "The Dalai Lama refers to meditation as 'internal disarmament.'"[5] We might imagine that he means internal peace. Thomas Troward who spent his career as a judge in India and wrote several profound books as a Western mystic, cites the reward of a regular meditation practice: "This, then, is the attitude of repose [meditation] in which we may enjoy all the beauties of science, literature and art or may peacefully commune with the spirit of nature…"[6] Anyone declining to at least explore meditation and the possibility of transformation or transcendence is obviously missing one of the great opportunities of the life we have been given.

Meditation might have originally had a close relationship with the process of developing of a new worldview or a paradigm shift. From his excellent book, *What the Buddha Taught*, we have Walpola Rahula: "The word meditation is a very poor substitute for the original term…which means culture or mental development…. It aims at cleansing the mind of impurities and disturbances, such as lustful desires, hatred, ill-will, indolence, worries and restlessness, skeptical doubts, and cultivating such qualities as concentration, awareness, intelligence, will, energy, the analytical faculty, confidence, joy, tranquility, leading finally to the attainment of highest wisdom which sees the nature of things as they are, and realizes the Ultimate Truth, Nirvana."[7] In other words, meditation is a way to examine and modify our feelings, beliefs, attitudes and values.

Rahula continues: "There are two forms of meditation. One is the development of mental concentration...leading up to the highest mystic stages...All these mystic states, according to the Buddha, are mind-created, mind produced, conditioned. They have nothing to do with Reality, Truth, Nirvana....He [the Buddha] considered these mystic-states only as 'happy living in this existence,' or 'peaceful living' and nothing more. He therefore discovered the other form of 'meditation' known as *vipassana* 'Insight' into the nature of things, leading to the complete liberation of mind, to the realization of the Ultimate Truth, Nirvana....It is an analytical method based on mindfulness, awareness, vigilance, observation."[8] This is a perfect description of the Point of Power Practice. Sakyong Mipham Rinpoche deepens our understanding with a simple definition: "Practice means 'bring it into experience.'"[9]

His Holiness, The Dalai Lama is well versed in modern scientific research as this description will affirm. "In Buddhism, this mental training is called *bhavana,* which is usually translated as 'meditation' in English. The original Sanskrit term *bhavana* carries connotations of cultivation, in the sense of cultivating familiarity with a given object, whether an external or an internal experience....Already experiments have shown that experienced meditators have more activity in the left frontal lobe, the part of the brain associated with positive emotions, such as happiness, joy, and contentment. These findings imply that happiness is something we can cultivate deliberately through mental training that affects the brain. [T]he Buddha himself argued that if one wishes to avoid certain types of results, one needs to change the conditions of one's state of mind (which normally give rise to particular habitual patterns of mental activity), one can change the traits of one's consciousness and the resulting attitudes and emotions."[10]

In fact, whether we call it "cultivating familiarity" as does the Dalai Lama or being the observer in the present moment, meditation involves quantifiable brain activity. Barry Boyce says, "For example, what metaphysical beliefs might you harbor that would make you wildly excited to learn that when people pay attention in meditation, they show the same pattern of brain activity as when they pay attention anywhere else?"[11]

Ken Wilber describes meditation in yet another way. "Meditation is, simply, a form of intensive attention training and its consequences, the major consequence being the triggering of an atypical sequence of adult development...According to the careful comparison of the traditions we have to conclude the following: *there is only one path, but it has several outcomes.* There are several kinds of enlightenment, although all free awareness from psychological structure and alleviate suffering."[12]

In the context of psychology, the observations of David Hawkins support our basic understanding of the dynamics of meditation. "Basic to the ego's continuance and capacity to dominate is its claim to authorship of all subjective experience. The 'I thought' is extremely quick in interjecting itself as the supposed cause of all aspects of one's life. This is difficult to detect except by intense focus of attention during meditation on the origination of the thought stream.... It becomes obvious [to the true self] that one is the witness of phenomena and not the cause or doer of them. The self, then, becomes that which is being witnessed rather than identifying with it as the witness or experiencer...."[13]

Hawkins continues, describing the function of the ego and its survival strategy in P-B: "The relinquishment of the ego self [false self] as one's central focus involves the letting go of all these layers of attachments and vanities, and one eventually comes face-to-face with the ego's primary function of control to ensure continuance and survival. Therefore, the ego clings to all its faculties because their basic purpose, to ensure its survival, is the 'reason' behind its obsession with gain, winning, learning, alliances, and accumulation of possessions, data, and skills. The ego has endless schemes for enhancing survival—some gross, some obvious, others subtle and hidden....The only simple task to be accomplished is to *let go of the identification with the ego as one's real self!*"[14]

Continuing in the language of psychology, Jack Engler adds that: "From the Buddhist point of view, concentration meditation induces transient states of happiness and conflict-free functioning by temporarily suppressing the operation of the drives [survival strategy] and the higher perceptual-intellectual functions [analysis, synthesis and evaluation]; but it is the insight [*Vipassana*] form of practice alone which liberates from suffering by bringing about enduring intra-psychic structural change....The meditator notes only the succession of thoughts, feelings [afflictive emotions] and sensations as these arise and pass away. In contrast to conventional psychotherapy work, no attention is paid to their individual content. Effectively, all stimuli are attended to equally without selection or censorship. Again in contrast to conventional psychotherapy, attention is kept 'bare' of any *reaction* [italics mine] to what is perceived....The aim is threefold: to come to know one's own mental processes; in this way to begin to have the power to shape or control them; and finally to gain freedom from the condition where one's psychic processes are unknown and uncontrolled."[15] This is a good description of why the Point of Power Practice is a simple and effective practice to bring about "intra-psychic structural change" or a paradigm shift.

Ken Wilber might also be speaking of a paradigm shift or changes in feelings, beliefs, attitudes and values in this next quote. In any case, his unique way of expressing it is refreshing. "Meditation frees the alert mind from external demands and also from the internal themes of unfinished business that pressure for planning and problem-solving. Like dreams, this special form of contemplative consciousness may allow a reworking of mental schemata and enduring attitudes in a unique way. Such changes in schemata may allow new conscious experiences, which then feed back to other changes. (Schemata are inner working models that contain information abstracted out of and generalized from earlier experiences. Mental development means elaborating existing schemata into new forms as well as nesting schemata into useful hierarchies.)"[16]

Remembering that repetition is necessary for deep and lasting reconditioning and transformation, let's review the foundational principles of meditation once again. We begin with the importance of focusing on the breath. We use the breath as the ground of present moment awareness because it is automatic. It requires no thought and is the perfect thing to observe or "witness" because as we practice observing the breath, we begin to create the separation from body, mind and emotions which is at the heart of a P-B identity. We are engaging in shifting our identity to that of the observer, to that which is free of false-self identification. "When we stop speaking and thinking," as Thich Nhat Hanh says, "and enjoy deeply in and out breath, we are enjoying being in our true home and we can touch deeply the wonders of life."[17]

We might not expect a Roman emperor to have understood this, but it is clear that Marcus Aurelius had profound insights of his own relating to meditation. "…those who do not observe the movements of their own minds must of necessity be unhappy."[18] The Edgar Cayce readings revealed the power of observers to change their past conditioning. "Only by cultivating an 'observer' consciousness—what Edgar Cayce called learning to 'stand aside and watch self pass by.' Simply being able to make that objective, non-judgmental observation creates a kind of 'observer energy' that can break old patterns."[19]

Our identity shift includes letting go of our attachment to thinking of ourselves as having a "self" separate from the rest of creation. Piero Ferrucci puts it this way: "In practicing Buddhist meditation, we discover to our surprise that the protagonist we thought ourselves to be does not exist; we are only a momentary, impersonal combination of mental states. In fact, there is nobody there to be tortured by problems and anxieties. From this perspective, everything takes place in a state of indescribable lightness, no longer fraught with dramas or terrors."[20] Such is the radical freedom inherent in Simple Reality.

Just as we realize that we are not a separate self, we come to let go of identifying with the mind and emotions. "The subtle difference with mindfulness is that 'while mindfulness recognizes the power of thoughts to shape our lives, it attends to those thoughts with acceptance. It doesn't try to get rid of anything. You realize that the part of you witnessing these thoughts and emotions is not the thoughts and emotions. It's your true nature. That's what heals."[21]

Steve Flowers has just reminded us that shifting from P-B to P-A is a process of becoming healthier both physically and mentally.

In experiencing Simple Reality we ultimately become more compassionate. Ken Wilber agrees: "Likewise, the soul is interior to the mind; it is *not inside* the mind—the only thing inside the mind is thoughts, which is why introspecting the mind never reveals the soul. As thoughts quiet down, however, the soul emerges interiorly vis-à-vis the mind, and therefore, can transcend the mind, see beyond it, escapes it. And likewise, spirit is not inside the soul, it is interior to the soul, transcending its limitations and forms. Apparently, then, theorists who claim that meditation is narcissistic imagine that meditators are going *inside* the mind; but they are rather going *interior* to it, and thus beyond it: less narcissistic, less subjectivistic, less self-centric, more universal, more encompassing, and thus ultimately more compassionate."[22]

Expanding meditation into our whole life with the Point of Power Practice helps recondition our reactive behaviors and supports the shift into P-A. Ken Wilber says: "It is important (particularly in our society, and particularly at this point in evolution) that one's spiritual practice be integrated into daily life and work.... Meditation, in my opinion, is not a means of digging back into the lower and repressed structures of the submergent-unconscious, it is a way of facilitating the emergence, growth, and development of the higher structures of consciousness. To confuse the two is to foster the reductionist notion, quite prevalent, that meditation is (at best) a regression in service of ego, whereas by design and practice it is a progression in the transcendence of ego.... Equally important, the student is instructed to remain mindful of each and every other activity he engages in throughout the day, as he does it. In effect then, meditation is continuous and is ideally carried on without a break from rising to sleeping. This continuity in practice is the single most important factor in developing and maintaining that high degree of concentration which facilitates the development of insight."[23]

The ultimate goal of all human activity is represented by the many statues of the Buddha sitting in peaceful repose. Remember

Nissargadatta's: Do nothing. Have nothing. Know nothing. Dilgo Khentse Rinpoche helps us remember that "The Buddha said, 'My practice is the practice of non-practice.' That means a lot. Give up all struggle. Allow yourself to rest."[24] Struggle is, of course, reaction pure and simple. Spiritual practices are all too often a form of reaction. To respond is to do nothing. That is true transcendence.

And finally, Joseph Campbell helps us keep a wholesome perspective in living a life with awareness. "And what then is finally the best austerity, what is the best discipline? The best discipline is to enjoy your friends. Enjoy your meals. Realize what play is. Participation in the play, in the play of life. This is known as *mahasuka,* the Great Delight."[25] Meditation is ultimately a healthy and joyful human activity and should not be undertaken as a burdensome and difficult task.

Chapter Fourteen

Present Moment

*We Have The Power To Transcend All Problems,
All Suffering, All Delusion – We Are Free*

> *The end of our exploring will be to arrive at where we
> started and to know the place for the first time.*
> T.S. Eliot

Paraphrasing Eliot's line of poetry to be consistent with a deeper understanding of what actually happens, we would have to say that in the present moment we arrive at the place we never left and *experience* it for the first time. In the language of Eastern spirituality, the ultimate human attainment is awareness and equanimity—that is to say, experiencing reality as it really is and behaving or accepting that reality without reaction. In so doing, we become a Buddha, an "awakened one." In the present moment we have transcended reincarnation, transmigration of souls and all other primitive attempts to answer the first Great Question—Where am I? Where we are in the present moment is P-A, beyond beginnings and endings in the eternal Now. We have transcended fear and suffering and entered the endless experience of compassion, freedom, peace, joy and happiness.

By definition "presence," being the essence of P-A, cannot be described in words since it is beyond the intellect. Words can only lead us in the general direction of Simple Reality, toward an experience of the Now. If words are to be used we would best leave that up to the poets, who, speaking from the heart, can elicit the "feeling" that accompanies our entry into the present moment. An exception would be the "poetic" prose of Emerson. "It has been said that 'common souls pay with what they do, nobler souls with that which they are.' And why? Because a profound nature awakens in us by its actions and words, by its very looks and manner, the same power and beauty that a gallery of sculpture or of pictures addresses."¹

> *Give me insight into to-day, and you may have the antique and future worlds.*
> Emerson

As Emerson indicated, art and beauty in all its forms can lead us toward an experience of the present moment. The editors of *Great Books of the Western World* also found that to be so when looking at Dostoevsky's great novel and then commenting on the Now. "When Dimmler in *War and Peace* tells Natasha that 'it is hard for us to imagine eternity,' she replies that it does not seem hard to her—that eternity 'is now today, and it will be tomorrow, and always, and was there yesterday and the day before…'…These and similar attempts may not succeed as much as the insight that if we could hold the present moment still, or fix the fleeting instant, we could draw an experience of the eternal from the heart of time. 'The *now* that stands still,' Aquinas writes, 'is said to make eternity according to our apprehension. For just as the apprehension of time is caused in us by the fact that we apprehend the flow of the *now*, so the apprehension of eternity is caused in us by our apprehending the *now* standing still.'"²

Awareness is not about the "attainment" of consciousness but the "un-attainment" of unconsciousness or of shifting our attention from "form" to "field"—from "noise" to "silence." We do not have to do anything to attain awareness—just stop doing that which distracts us from our essential nature; just stop "reacting." To put it in religious language we could say: "I am not a human being seeking my way to God; rather God is unfolding and revealing It's own being in me."

Thomas Merton said: "'Being spiritual is something most people worry about when they are so busy with something else that they think they ought to be spiritual.' This is why the experience of the spiritual foundations of reality is described as a 'realization' or 'revelation,' that is, the awareness of something that already exists."³ The "something that already exists" that Merton speaks of is Simple Reality.

What you are aware of you are in control of. What you are *not* aware of is in control of you. One of the lowest levels of awareness is adherence to a set of rules (commandments or precepts) from an outside authority. In such a paradigm we face condemnation and sanctions from priests, ministers, masters and gurus. This is why Christianity (the Ten Commandments) and Buddhism (the Eightfold Path) do not often result in transformation of human behavior. If we condemn ourselves for breaking a precept, we suffer guilt and shame about the past. If we can't seem to live up to religious sanctions, we have fear and anxiety about the future. Either way, precepts and commandments make it less likely that we can spend much time in the present moment. If we take full responsibility for our own behavior and follow the wisdom and compassion found in the Now, we are rewarded by the power inherent in accessing our own interior awareness. We have transcended fear.

Fear is not of the present, but only of the past and future.
A Course in Miracles

"A mind in the present moment," says Peter Russell, "is free to experience *what is*. This does not imply that one no longer takes any notice of the past nor considers the future. There is still much to learn from the past, and there are still innumerable ways we can influence the future and thus improve the quality of our lives and the lives of others. The difference is that, once liberated from its state of trance, the mind is no longer lost in fruitless concerns about things that happened in the past, nor is it caught up in anxieties about what may or may not happen in the future. Instead, we can focus more fully on the task at hand."[4]

Russell's experience is further confirmed by the 13th century German theologian and mystic, Meister Eckhart. "There exists only the present moment…a Now which always and without end is itself new…. There is no yesterday nor any tomorrow, but only Now, as it was a thousand years ago and as it will be a thousand years hence."[5]

And yet we have to be wary of the mind that Russell speaks of – remember the limitations of the intellect? The present moment is not experienced by the mind but by our intuitive self beyond the mind. The Eastern teachers often have a more profound grasp of the distinction between paradigms A and B. Tulku Urgyen Rinpoche says, "If you believe there is a thing called mind, it is just a thought. If you believe there is no thing called mind, it's just another thought. Your natural state, free of any kind of thought about it—that is Buddha nature. In ordinary sentient beings, this natural state is carried away by thinking, caught up in thought. Involvement in thinking is like a heavy chain. The moment you shatter the chain of thinking, you are free from the three realms of *samsara* [the reactions associated with craving, aversion and ignorance, and the resultant suffering]."[6]

We can further refine this distinction between thinking and awareness with the help of Henepola Gunaratana from his book, *Mindfulness in Plain English.*

Awareness...
- is not thinking
- does not compare experiences
- precedes thought in the chain of perception
- is always in the present moment
- is being present without the ego
- involves observing all mental, physical and emotional phenomena
- involves being an objective observer without resistance
- is an interior experience unconcerned with the world outside[7]

Transcending P-B involves penetrating the heart of P-A. The Buddhist worldview and that of P-A contain three foundational principles – *Dukkha*, *Anicca*, and *Anatta*. Awareness involves an experience of *Dukkha* (suffering) meaning that all things in the sensory or experiential world are ultimately unsatisfactory. An experience of *Anicca* (impermanence) means that nothing in our experience lasts. And an experience of *Anatta* (no "me") means that there is no personal entity, no unchanging "I" but only ever-changing processes. There is no "watcher" only the process of "watching." And finally, awareness involves seeing reality as it really is which means among other things that awareness is *Appamada* which means "the absence of madness." The words in italics are Pali words, the vernacular language that Buddha spoke.

Even from the "world beyond" we can find confirmation of the present moment in the voice of "Seth" as channeled by Jane Roberts. "You rule your experience from the focal point of your present, where your beliefs directly intercept with the body and the physical world on the one hand and the invisible world on the other. This applies to the individuals, societies, races and nations, and to sociological, biological and psychic activities."[8]

The moment we start to talk, many of us leave the Now and fall into the slumber of thinking far away from the blissful state of present moment peace. As we have already noted, it takes a poet to transcend the inadequate expressive power of mere words woven by the intellect.

> His arms a pillow,
> The sky his canopy,
> The genial breeze a fan,
> His lamp the autumn moon,
> And dispassion his wife.
> Thus the sage rejoices,
> And like some noble monarch
> Reclines at ease, and in peace.
>   Bhartrihari [9]

The "feeling" of being present is illusive and for most of us will only be experienced a few times in a lifetime, in a fleeting moment that psychologist Abraham Maslow has called a "peak experience." In seeking this experience (a glimpse of P-A), we are transcending craving and aversion of all kinds, even what we tend to regard as desirable sensations. A few descriptions of this experience from several different cultures and sources are helpful. Listen with the heart and not the head.

> *In proud for feeling of such lofty bliss,*
> *I now enjoy the highest Moment—this!*
> Goethe—*Faust*

In her own language Toni Packer is speaking of peak experience. "The emergence and blossoming of understanding, love and intelligence has nothing to do with any tradition, no matter how ancient or impressive—it has nothing to do with time. It happens completely on its own when a human being questions, wonders, listens, and looks without getting stuck in fear, pleasure, and pain."[10]

> *When consciousness is no longer totally absorbed by*
> *thinking, some of it remains in its formless,*
> *unconditioned state. This is inner space.*
> Eckhart Tolle [11]

The present moment is understood and practiced to some degree by the mystics of the world's major religions. It was the influence of the Hindu/Buddhist tradition that finally opened the eyes of western philosophers such as Emerson and Thomas Troward to the importance of exploring the deeper nature of reality. A contemporary mystic, Eckhart Tolle, author of the popular *The Power of Now*, is a modern case in point. Gaylon Ferguson in an article about Tolle describes this influence. "It was only later, after reading spiritual texts such as *A Course in Miracles* and meeting with Theravadin Buddhist monks in England, that he began to call this [his] transformation *awakening*. But again, he seems as pleased to note that in Hinduism and Buddhism this is called *enlightenment* as to note that in the teachings of Jesus it is *salvation.*"[12]

Ken Wilber describing and quoting the Spanish Christian mystic, Teresa of Avila, says, "And here Teresa uses perhaps her most famous metaphor. Prior to this transformative absorption, the unregenerate [false] self (or ego) is, says Teresa, like a silkworm. But one taste of union (literally, just a single experience of this, she says however brief), and the self is changed forever. One taste of absorption in Uncreate Spirit, and the worm emerges a butterfly. As we might put it, the ego dies and the soul emerges. ('All mean egotism vanishes; the currents of Universal Being circulate through me; I am part or parcel of God.')..."[13]

Joseph Campbell brings the perspective of the mythologist to the Gnostic Gospel of Thomas. "Here Jesus says, 'The Kingdom will not come by expectation. They will not say, See here, see there. The Kingdom of the Father is spread upon the earth and men do not see it.' That's what's known as the Hermetic Gnosticism—*bodhi,* in Sankrit. Change the perspective of your eyes, and you see the whole world before you is radiant....In other words the coming is right here, now, in the world, and not at all something to wait for, not for a historical experience."[14]

> *Do any human beings ever realize life while they live it?—every, every minute?*
>   Emily in "Our Town" by Thornton Wilder

One of America's original contributions to world culture is New Thought. The origin of New Thought can be traced back to the mystic P.P. Quimby born in Lebanon, New Hampshire in 1802. Quimby clearly understood the importance of the present moment when he, in speaking of death, said that it was "'an external incident, of which man need not stand in fear. Rather once having accepted the thought of eternity now,' ...man might remain calm, poised, free, and overcome the 'illusion of sense experience with its manifold bondages.'"[15]

> "Awareness of the world *as it is* makes the world new."
>   Michael Adam [16]

Although I can't always follow what Ken Wilber is saying, my intuition tells me he is onto something. In any case he expresses it in an endlessly fascinating way. (The Eastern tradition uses the word "emptiness" for the present moment.) "Emptiness is neither a Whole nor a Part nor a Whole/Part. Emptiness is the reality of which all Wholes and all parts are simply manifestations. In Emptiness I do not become Whole, nor do I realize that I am merely a Part of some Great Big Whole. Rather, in Emptiness I become the opening or clearing in which all wholes and all parts arise eternally. I-I am the groundless

Ground, the empty Abyss, that never enters the stream of endless IOUs;.... Not in Emptiness, but as Emptiness, I am released from the fate of a never-ending addition of parts, and I stand free as the Source and Suchness of the glorious display. I taste the sky and swallow whole the Kosmos, and nothing is added to me; I disappear in a million forms and nothing is subtracted; I rise as the sun to greet my own day, and nothing moves at all."[17] Ken Wilber the Kosmic poet. I like it.

Let's have another taste. "Indeed, indeed: let the self-contraction relax into the empty ground of its own awareness, and let it there quietly die. See the Kosmos arise in its place, dancing madly and divine, self-luminous and self-liberating, intoxicated by a Light that never dawns nor ceases. See the worlds arise and fall, never caught in time and turmoil, transparent images shimmering in the radiant Abyss. Watch the mountain walk on water, drink the Pacific in a single gulp, blink and a billion universes rise and fall, breathe out and create a Kosmos, breathe in and watch it dissolve."

And another: "Let the ecstasy overflow and outshine the loveless self, driven mad with the torments of its self-embracing ways, hugging mightily *samsara's* spokes of endless agony, and sing instead triumphantly with Saint Catherine, 'My being is God, not by simple participation, but by a true transformation of my Being. My *me* is God!' And let the joy sing with Dame Julian, 'See I am God! See! I am in all things! See! I do all things!' And let the joy shout with Hakuin, 'This very body is the Body of Buddha! And this very land the Pure Land!'..."

He's on a roll, can't stop now! "And comes to rest that Godless search, tormented and tormenting. The knot in the Heart of the Kosmos relaxes to allow its only God, and overflows the Spirit ravishes and enraptured by the lost and found Beloved. And gone the Godless destiny of death and desperation, and gone the madness of a life committed to uncare, and gone the tears and terror of the brutal days and endless nights where time alone would rule."

And now we "feel" the last crashing wave wash over us and we have some idea of the experience of the present moment. "And I-I rise to taste the dawn, and find that love alone will shine today. And the Shining says: to love it all, and love it madly, and always endlessly, and ever fiercely, to love without choice and thus enter the All, to love it mindlessly and thus be the All embracing the only and radiant Divine: now as Emptiness, now as Form, together and forever, the Godless search undone, and love alone will shine today."[18] Now *that* is what *feeling* the present moment is all about!

You might not think science would have anything to say about the present moment but some interesting research is being done. For example this observation by Diane Powell: "Some people have conditions such as autism that shift the balance between local and non-local processes by knocking out the functioning of the neo-cortex. The rest of us can decrease this classical dominance by such mind-quieting practices as meditation. Hence, as we become more consciously aware or awake, we use non-local processes more and more. Along the way, we will progressively see the world less abstractly. We will see it more as it really is."[19]

But, of course, the present moment is not about what's "out there" as Thoreau began to intuit during his stay at Walden Pond. Alfred Tauber said that "Thoreau is clear, as Emerson seldom was, about the location of meaning and value. He is saying that it does not reside in the natural facts or in social institutions or in anything 'out there,' but in consciousness."[20]

Philosophers have not had much to say about the present moment perhaps because it is not "head stuff," too concrete, too experiential. Wilber explores why this might be so. "This 'emptiness' is not a theory. Even less is it 'poetry' (which I have often heard). Nor is it a philosophical suggestion. It is a direct apprehension (direct 'experience' is not quite right), since it is free of the duality of subject and object, and since it never enters the stream of time and thus is never 'experiential' in any typical sense—free of thoughts, free of dualities, free of time and temporal succession..."[21]

Psychologists, on the other hand, have a field day with speculations about the nature and significance of the Now. Rollo May, for example: "But the more awareness one has—that is, the more he experiences himself as the acting, directing agent in what he is doing—the more alive he will be and the more responsive to the present moment."[22]

We have learned that we enter the present moment when we are in response, rather than reacting to what is happening in our mental or physical experience. Ken Wilber puts on his psychologists hat: "All the traditions agree that reactivity stops, although the fate of emotional reactions differs in each tradition....In any case, the human experience of suffering is altered because of the change in how information about emotions is processed....What the meditation texts claim is quite radical: nothing short of a life without the experience of emotional pain. Freud was more pessimistic about psychoanalysis, through which the interpretation of free associations might only replace neurotic suffering with ordinary human unhappiness. The meditation masters have picked up where Freud left off. In the words of the Buddha, 'If there's one thing only I teach you, it is the end of suffering.' Disciplined deployment of attention [Point of Power Practice], which may permanently alter human information-processing, may alleviate all traces of everyday unhappiness."[23] Worthwhile, I would say, this business of a new story, a new identity and "a life without emotional pain." We should try it, don't you think?

Chapter Fifteen

Peak Experience

*Simple Reality Is Our Natural State And
Most Of Us Have Been There For At Least A Short Visit*

There is no difference between the present moment and peak experience except that a peak experience is a spontaneous human occurrence that is not created by the "experiencer." It will be of value to examine this event from a slightly different perspective than that used in Chapter Fourteen.

The psychologist Abraham Maslow used peak experience to describe what we call the present moment, the experience of the Now. As a spontaneous happening of the present moment, a peak experience could also be labeled a theophany, an epiphany, flow, ecstasy or an experience of the numinous. "A comprehension or perception of reality by means of a sudden intuitive realization," is a good definition of a peak experience. It is an experience of Simple Reality, "the highest human attainment possible for any of us," would be a conventional way of expressing it which is a problematic definition because it is not an "attainment" at all but rather the absence of any attainment. Also related to being in the present moment are the hypnogogic or hypnopompic states, epiphanies involving the implicate order or the akashic record and the experience of our intuition. And finally in the most simple and pragmatic way we can describe a peak experience as when we have chosen to respond rather than react to what is happening.

"Not until Maslow codified the benefits of the peak experience, as well as what he called the Being-values (i.e., values which correspond to the awareness of the transcendent realm), did researchers, educators and the various helping professions begin paying closer attention to the attitudes, behaviors and values of human health."[1] Notice how close Marsha Sinetar's descriptors are to our definition of worldview: feelings/emotions, beliefs, attitudes and values. A peak experience is a connection to our natural state in P-A, a spontaneous transcendence of the old narrative.

Seth stresses the important realization that peak experiences are perfectly normal but not often sanctioned by our P-B story. "Natural 'mystical' experience, unclothed in dogma, is the original religious therapy that is so often distorted in ecclesiastical organizations, but it represents man's innate recognition of his oneness with the source of his own being, and of his own experience."[2]

A peak experience can have a powerful transformational effect. The great Russian novelist, Fyodor Dostoyevski, describes the experience of the perfection of Simple Reality. "I feel a perfect harmony in myself and my surroundings, and this sensation is so strong that for a few moments of such bliss I would give ten years of my life...perhaps my whole life."[3]

Arjuna Ardagh describes a peak experience calling it a "radical awakening." "Robert was out on an evening walk. He had been through a series of trials and tribulations over the previous several years, and his mood was blacker than the night. 'I am finished,' his mind announced. He still has trouble explaining what happened next. 'I was overcome by a sense of relief,' he reports, 'a sudden feeling of inexpressible freedom. I even began to laugh out loud. My body was filled with happiness, as if I were suddenly getting a joke I'd been missing. For the first time I was feeling really good for no reason at all. I was totally here, in this moment. I could feel the trees around me, and hear the sounds without having to listen to thoughts telling me things needed to be different in some way. Everything was being experienced but the 'me' was gone... you taste reality outside the limiting confines of the mind, when you know yourself to be limitless, much bigger than—yet still containing—the body, beyond birth and death, eternally free.... It is the moment when you can intuit the real potential of life, free from the incessant machinery of complaint and ambition... Such awakening can leave an imprint on the body and psyche. You are left with a deep knowing of the perfection of things, even when they are going wrong.'"[4] When we seem to have "hit bottom" in our life's journey, a peak experience is often triggered as a sort of reminder message of our true identity. "Do not despair, you have mistaken your nightmare for reality," it seems to say.

This happened to Ramakrishna when "…at one point in his life he was in such anguish that nothing held meaning for him. On the verge of suicide and in a moment of madness, he ran to fetch a sword. But at that very moment his mind was enlightened." In his own words "It was as if houses, doors, temples and everything else vanished! And what I saw was an infinite shoreless sea of light; a sea that was consciousness."[5]

Psychologist C. G. Jung explained peak experience in this way "[He]… said that the numinosum 'was the influence of an invisible presence that causes a peculiar alteration in consciousness.'"[6] Reading in the *Abstracts of the Collected Works of C. G. Jung* we find a more detailed description: "…psychic experiences as spontaneous expressions of religious or mystical truths make them difficult to explain in purely scientific terms. Nonetheless, it is contended that numinous experiences, whether they are interpreted as merely pathological or as divine inspirations, derive from an overwhelming breakthrough of unconscious material into consciousness. The metaphysical interpretations ascribed to these psychic happenings are seen as consciously elaborated hypotheses; gods, then, are not external forces but images projected by the psychoid realm. The validity of the inner experience of transcendental reality remains, but as a product of man himself."[7]

Peak experiences also have the power to take us beyond the illusion of the ego or the false self. "The experience of the objective fact is all important, because it denotes the presence of something which is not I," says Jung, "yet is still psychical. Such an experience can reach a climax where it becomes an experience of God."[8] Jung, being a Christian, speaks in religious terms.

Concluding this chapter, Marsha Sinetar says, "The peak experience conditions the personality to death because during it, the individual 'ego' (i.e., separate sense, the 'I') vanishes. With this vanishing goes the fear of death, since the ego, the I, is what keeps those fears in place, believing as it does that there is a death—that is to say, a no-life condition—to fear. When the personality joins something so much larger, eternal, infinite—even with the disappearance of the separate sense of self—the fear of death goes."[9] Obviously, peak experiences give us an insight into a truer, more profound reality and could be a valuable resource that our culture dare not continue to ignore.

Chapter Sixteen

Silence, Simplicity And Solitude

Becoming Quiet, Slowing Down And Spending Time Alone Can Be Transformational

Fundamental changes in lifestyle are possible with the support of the principles of Simple Reality. The benefits of beginning the process of change are immediate and cumulative. Experience the freedom from self-destructive, conditioned behaviors and the power of self-reliance.

Silence

Meister Eckhhart said that there is nothing in the world that resembles God so much as silence. Silence surrounds every beautiful sound or we could not experience it. Perhaps that is why sitting meditation is the universal practice used to approach and experience Simple Reality—the still, silent voice within. Even thought forms are a type of "noise." Serenity, joy and compassion are "feelings" found in the present moment because they are our essence, they compose our natural state of being—the field out of which our form emerges. Silence is very difficult to attain in the modern world. Contemplatives have found the courage to turn from the outside world where the senses are enthralled, to their interior space to explore a world apart from the preoccupations of the body, the security of the mind and the sensations of the emotions.

> *There are those among you who seek the talkative through fear of being alone.*
> Kahlil Gibran [1]

Thinking and talking can be one of the many strategies that we employ as a way of distracting ourselves from the existential pain of

P-B. All strategies involved in the seeking of security, sensation and power we know to be futile. Silence is a strategy, however, that works. "In May 1957, Jung wrote to Gustav Schmaltz saying that solitude was for him 'a fount of healing' which made life still worth living. 'Talking is often a torment for me and I need many days of silence to recover from the futility of words.'"[2]

> *You talk when you cease to be at peace with your thoughts.*
> Kahlil Gibran [3]

The simple act of quieting the mind, becoming silent, focusing on our inner calm will allow the Simple Reality of our natural state to emerge. "Place yourself in the middle of the stream of power and wisdom which animates all whom it floats, and you are without effort impelled to truth, to right and a perfect contentment."[4] This is how Emerson described the effect of silence.

The relationship between evolution and context is instructive at this point. A child is born with the capacity to learn language, but if there is no one in the environment speaking a language that capacity will not be realized and the child will remain mute. The research of Joseph Chilton Pearce supports the importance of the evolutionary readiness as well as willingness of humanity to transcend its current narrative and behavior.

Before humankind or any other aspect of creation for that matter could evolve, the necessary environment had to exist. For example, our brain is a three-part organ. Before it could evolve from the reptilian brain (the inner core of our brain) to the limbic brain, the necessary evolutionary environment had to exist. Before the limbic brain (the simple sensory-motor brain focused on survival) could evolve to having the ability to think and have emotions, nature's program for that shift had to be evolved. The neo-cortex, the third part of our brain, gave us our potential to "feel" sympathy and to do creative thinking. We now have the potential to transcend to the next level of human consciousness which will enable us to live on this planet in a sustainable manner. The context that will support that shift is P-A. The practice that will support each individual involves entering into the ineffable space that is surrounded by silence.[5]

Simplicity

> *Life is so short, we must really slow down.*
> Thich Nat Hanh

Simplicity is one of three elements of the formula for how a P-A centered life is lived. That formula is: S+S+S=S or simplicity plus solitude plus silence equals serenity. Living in the present moment our life becomes a meditation and these are some of the characteristics of the contemplative life. From *The Meditations of Marcus Aurelius*, the Roman emperor/philosopher appreciated simplicity even though his life was far from simple. "Occupy thyself with few things, says the philosopher, if thou wouldst be tranquil."[6]

> *There is a pervasive form of contemporary violence...* [and that is] *activism and overwork. The rush and pressure of modern life are a form, perhaps the most common form, of its innate violence.*
> Thomas Merton

Contemplatives in a religious context in the past, whether living in ashrams, monasteries or convents, often were seeking refuge from the harsh world dominated by competition, materialism, pleasure seeking and violence. If they could find a paradigm offering solitude, a simple life and time for meditation and prayer then perhaps they could live a life of response instead of reaction. Such a life of transcendence is what we all seek but most of us will have to find a way to do it in our day-to-day life. It helps if we have a plan. Simple Reality is such a plan.

Solitude

> *When from our better selves we have too long been parted by the hurrying world...*
> Wordsworth

William Wordsworth goes on to say more about the desirability of solitude: "'How gracious, how benign, is Solitude' especially when it has an 'appropriate human centre.'"[7] That appropriate human center is a wholesome context like Simple Reality. In the present moment we are connected to the implicate order from which flows the serenity, the "feeling" of which Wordsworth speaks.

> *I now bask in the solitude that was so painful to me in my youth.*
> Albert Einstein

Chapter Seventeen

Absolute And Relative

Understanding The Distinction Between Reality And Illusion Can Free Humanity From Our Ongoing Self-Destruction

Be ye perfect, even as your Father which is in heaven is perfect.
                        Matthew 5:38-48.

We experience the Absolute when we are consciously in the present moment. We experience the relative when we are unconsciously living in the past or the future. To be present is to experience the perfection of the life we have been given. All of creation is perfect and being part of that creation, we are also perfect. There is no need to improve upon creation, only to learn to live in the present moment so that we can experience that perfection. Our natural state is conscious awareness of the Absolute. Nothing has to be done, acquired or learned to attain this awareness.

Ken Wilbur speaks about the importance of being able to embrace paradox without conflict as a critical ability if we are to attain present moment awareness. "So psychological as well as spiritual (or meditative) development is helpful in unfolding one's own deeper potentials—you can develop virtually everything from moral response to meditative absorption. But all of those are of the relative, manifest realm—the realm of *samsara* [suffering]—and the whole point of enlightenment is to step off that cycle altogether. This is why Vedanta and *dzogchen* also maintain that, in the last analysis, meditation will not itself bring final spiritual awareness (because such awareness, being ever present, has no beginning in time and thus cannot be entered: you cannot enter that which you have never left)."[1] As I said in the introductory paragraph, as we enter into the realm of the Now, we leave conventional logic behind and transcend to a more profound mode of knowing.

> *You arrive at the place you never left and see* [experience] *it for the first time.*
> T.S. Eliot

The thinking mind is unable to describe absolute truth. It can be described as "emptiness" because, to the mind which deals with concepts, it has no form. When there is no sense of self, the mind can rest in peace and quiet. Self-realization is non-verbal, non-conceptual so the mind cannot grasp it. The Buddha taught in terms of the relationship between the relative and the Absolute, conventional truth and ultimate truth. Hinduism and Buddhism deal with this relationship little understood in the West.

Many people have spiritual practices such as prayer and meditation. These practices are rarely successful in leading to the shift from P-B to P-A. That's because few practitioners realize that the purpose of any profoundly conceived religious or spiritual practice is to become present, to see reality as it really is.

The meaning of the term "enlightenment" has proved confusing and illusive for many people but we will use it simply to mean being in the Now. "From the perspective of the absolute nature," says Dzogchen Ponlop Rinpoche, "we say that things are empty and do not have true existence. However, from the perspective of relative reality, from the conventional point of view, things do exist in the nature of interdependence.... With the wisdom of knowing who we truly are, Absolute and relative compassion will manifest naturally toward all sentient beings and benefit them extensively. That is what we call achieving complete enlightenment."[2]

The absolute can only be "felt" not detected by the five senses. It has no form and a term like "heart-felt" is the closest we can come to that which is beyond words. And yet the feeling associated with the present moment is the most vivid experience that we can have as human beings. The experience of the Now is in fact the only thing that has ultimate reality. In his book, *What the Buddha Taught,* Walpola Rahula says: "According to Buddhism, the Absolute Truth is that there is nothing absolute in the world, that everything is relative, conditioned and impermanent, and that there is no unchanging, everlasting, absolute substance like Self, Soul...."[3]

We face another paradox trying to talk about that which cannot be talked about and so we can only choose words that point to the Now or help deliver us into the heart-felt experience of P-A. Clive Johnson says, "This absorption leads to *Samadhi* [the Now], an experience which cannot be described. It is beyond *is* and *is not.* There, there is neither happiness nor misery, neither light nor darkness. All is infinite Being—inexpressible."[4]

The following table can be useful in verbally distinguishing the absolute from the relative.

Absolute	**Relative**
Essence	Ego
True self	False self
Intuition	Thinking
Feelings (freedom, joy, peace, happiness)	Emotions (always afflictive, like jealousy)
Being	Having, knowing and doing
Following our bliss	Habituated behavior
	Collective unconscious
	Collective consciousness (like group-think)
	Shadow
	Models, trainings, classes and seminars
	Community participation

Our conditioning related to the false self survival strategy can hypnotize us into thinking that our identity is related to seeking security, sensations and power. In fact we are powerless in that "seeking" state and are engaged in the endeavors of having, knowing and doing. So much effort and suffering to no avail. We might just as well relax and enjoy what amounts to a very short life on this planet. Again, Clive Johnson: "Everything is ours already—infinite purity, freedom, love and power.... You know in your inmost heart that many of your limited ideas—this humbling of yourself, and praying and weeping to imaginary beings—are superstitions." [5]

Understanding the distinction between the Absolute and the relative in the context of everyday life is necessary. For example, how do we explain why a perfect being in a perfect narrative becomes ill? Jan Chozen Bays answers this critically important question. "...from a relative point of view we can't really avoid illness. It happens. On an absolute level, however, there is a fundamental state of mind that is open and natural and healthy. It is possible even in the midst of intense illness and the dying process to contact this fundamentally pure and wholesome state of mind. However, many people confuse contacting that fundamental healthy state of mind with using it to avoid disease, as opposed to letting it allow you to feel better about the illness that inevitably happens."[6]

It is a mind-boggling challenge for most of us to shift from trying to succeed in the world through intellectual understanding to "feeling" the perfection of a world wherein we are already a smashing success no matter what is happening. "Now, what is called the Self Absolute or the un-manifest ground of being is that deepest part of human consciousness that, because it abides beyond time and space," says Andrew Cohen, "beyond creation itself, does not care at all about what's happening here in the realm of manifestation. It's always free from anything that's ever happened here and always is at rest. Infinite peace is its nature. So whatever does happen in our world, in the manifest realm, has no effect on that deepest part of our self. Birth or death, Big Bang or no Big Bang."[7]

"Because your will is free you can accept what has already happened at any time you choose, and only then will you realize that it was always there."[8] As the *Course in Miracles* emphasizes, you are not free to choose the curriculum, or even the form in which you will learn it. You are free, however, to decide when you want to learn it. And as you accept it, it is already learned.

Shifting from P-B to P-A is a life-long process because we live side-by-side with our false self which will not magically vanish. The inertia of the false-self conditioning is too strong to simply disappear. However, this is not a problem, only an opportunity that we are perfectly capable of taking advantage of. I remember when the Dalai Lama gave a brief Q & A session at a weekend seminar that I was attending at Naropa University in Boulder. He was asked if he ever got angry. He answered, "Yes, but it is not a problem." I think he meant that he did not "react" but let the emotion pass and returned to the present moment. Even Jesus lost his temper and experienced the reaction of afflictive emotions on a number of occasions. He was angry when he drove the money lenders from the temple, he was rude to his mother at Cana, annoyed with his apostles many times, and he cursed and killed the fig tree. So we shouldn't feel too disappointed when we forget to breathe and count to ten, when we react instead of responding in the Now. It is human and natural to move back and forth between the relative and the Absolute, but it is "divine" to be aware that we are doing it.

Notice the following variety of sources that support the basic thesis that all of creation is perfect, here and now, just as it is and that we know it at the level of our heart-felt inner wisdom.

First, Thom Hartmann in his book *The Last Hours of Ancient Sunlight,* concludes, "There is nothing we need to get that is not already right here, right now, in this very body and mind as it is.... To seek for something other than 'just this' implies that something is missing, that we are not complete somehow."[9]

Next, Jaimal Yogis reminds us that concepts around the notion of "good and bad" cannot be found in P-A. "One of the highest insights in the Mahayana and Vajrayana Buddhist traditions is to realize that *samsara* (suffering) is, in fact, nirvana: that there is no need to escape because everything is originally pure and perfect."[10]

If knowledge of the distinction between the Absolute and the relative is inherent in each human being, we should not be surprised to find it mentioned in the oldest of the great religions, Hinduism. This description is found in the book *The Mystic Heart* by Wayne Teasdale. "The Hindu tradition's mysticism issues from its sustained contemplation of the Absolute, which Hindus name *Brahman*. Through higher states of meditation, mystic seers contact Brahman, which then opens the way to inner awareness of the self, or *Atman*, the immanent presence of the Brahman within all beings and every particle of reality. Atman is Brahman, and Brahman is Atman. They aren't concepts but pure mystical realization."[11]

A student of Hindu cosmology, the American philosopher Emerson, understood the problem in being mesmerized by the false self survival strategy. "According to Emerson, man is 'by his nature as unconditioned, as pure, as perfect and alone as the infinite. But he doesn't know it and the smoke screen of his own conditioning forever fogs him'"[12]

When we understand the difference between the Absolute and the relative we have laid the foundation upon which we can proceed toward that all-important insight that will awaken our deepest connection with the good, the true and the beautiful, that quickening of the heart that will deliver us to the kingdom where joy, happiness and compassion reign.

Chapter Eighteen

Transcendence

We Must Increase Our Understanding Of Where We Are Going In The Paradigm Shift And The Obstacles To Getting There

This chapter on transcendence will contrast the simplicity (intuition) of P-A with the complexity (intellect) of P-B. The following paragraph defines transcendence in the context of P-A.

The transcendent is the Absolute and in biblical language is referred to in the Book of Matthew. *Be ye perfect, even as your Father which is in heaven is perfect.* (Matthew 5:38-48.) Transcendence is simply an experience of the present moment, independent of materiality. It is the state of being we experience in Simple Reality. It can further be characterized as being in response rather than in reaction, or experiencing compassion rather than fear. It is also being free of the craving and aversion that accompanies the pursuit of security, sensation and power. To maintain the state of transcendence usually requires the Point of Power Practice to confront and combat the old conditioning that defines P-B.

What you have just read is a simple explanation of transcendence. Nothing more need be added to make it complete. Simplicity is the essence of P-A. Contrast this simple explanation of transcendence with the following more detailed and complex exploration that the intellect is fond of.

But before we begin, remember that there is nothing wrong with enjoying exercising the mind with problem solving or creating theories, models and constructs. Nothing wrong, that is, unless we fail to distinguish between intellectual activities as P-B endeavors in contrast with P-A creation which flows from the inner wisdom, the intuition of the present moment. The important principle here is that the intellect serves and is subordinate to intuition. At this point you perhaps are beginning to see the advantage of Simple Reality. I chose that name because P-A is just that—simple. Now let's have fun observing the workings of some of the world's most profound minds relating to the subject of transcendence.

Transcendence is fraught with paradox because it cannot be "achieved" in the conventional sense and yet certain things seem to help achieve it. Or as a Buddhist teacher put it: "Enlightenment is an accident: meditation makes you accident prone." This distinction was dealt with in the context of the history of Christianity in the controversy over grace versus works. Does a Christian gain heaven by the grace of God or by how he lives his life? This argument takes one to the heart of the identity of God. Is God's love conditional, that is to say, does one have to earn that love by "works" or is God's love freely given and one enters heaven on account of God's "grace" regardless of one's behavior? That debate continues among Christians, but the Hindu teacher Nisargadatta Maharaj came down on the side of grace with his pronouncement that one has to "know nothing, have nothing, do nothing" to attain transcendence. Nisargadatta believed that grace is our natural state.

If we don't feel safe on the journey to higher states of consciousness, we will abort the journey—it will be too threatening. The Einstein question (Is the Universe friendly?) must be answered affirmatively before we depart toward the frontier of consciousness. So the change that we are advocating takes place in two dimensions—the Absolute and the relative—P-A and P-B.

One of the pitfalls of the intellect in solving problems is that it has trouble telling symptoms from problems and I gave an example of that in Chapter One relating to the "War on Drugs." Secondly, the intellect has historically been fond of "reductionism," i.e. breaking down form and phenomena into the smallest possible components. The pursuit of the atom in physics and then waves and particles is an example. This has not been a waste of time in science since practical results can be achieved by the intellect but it is not possible for the intellect to comprehend ultimate reality or Simple Reality. The following example of this is an analysis of the path toward transcendence, a process separated into four stages.

These distinctions address the paradox of transcendence being a process and not being a process, or being stages as opposed to states of consciousness. Ken Wilber identifies the four stages and the three states: "Those stages represent one's identity, moving from an identification merely with 'me' [egocentric] to an identification with 'us' [ethnocentric] to an identification with 'all of us' [worldcentric] to an identification with the 'All' [Kosmocentric]. As permanent realizations, those are *stages;* they develop and unfold.

"States on the other hand, can mean states of consciousness like waking, dreaming, deep sleep, and so on....For ordinary people in the waking state, the self they have is the ego. In the subtle or dream state, it's the soul or what you're calling the Authentic Self, which I refer to as the deeper psychic. And in the deep-sleep formless state, it's the Absolute Self. Now if we describe those three as...gross, subtle, causal, then those are the three major, or basic, selves that every human being possesses. We have a gross self, or ego, a subtle self, or soul or deeper psychic, and a causal, formless absolute or *atman* Self, a transcendental witness.... States are free; stages are earned.... But you have to be at least a world-centric stage of development or it's not going to stick."[1]

Transcendence is further complicated by being characterized as a three-stage process. Using the labels from Ken Wilber's model:

1. Translation (unconscious unconsciousness)

Translation consciousness sees the universe as fundamentally an unsafe place. Therefore, the false-self or ego creates a survival strategy investing all of its energy in the pursuit of security, sensation and power. By remaining unconscious and denying reality, the ego pretends that life is satisfactory. At a collective level, human institutions engage in lies, denial and secrets to maintain the illusion that all is well.

Translation is an intellectual activity and what is merely understood is not internalized. For example Arthur Miller describes why he couldn't write the play *A View from the Bridge* without first internalizing what it meant. "I saw that the reason I had not written it was that as a whole its meaning escaped me. I could not fit it into myself. It existed apart from me and seemed not to express anything within me."[2] After entering the present moment in the creative process, internalizing the meaning, he was able to complete the play.

2. Transformation (conscious unconsciousness)

The intellect can facilitate the process of transformation, can help us begin the journey toward transcendence, but cannot deliver us to the destination.

Thomas Moore further defines the process of transformation. "Our developmental models of a human life account for progress but not major shifts in being. Linear thinking, so much a part of modern life, affects the way we understand our very lives.... We imagine growing like a skyscraper under construction, reaching to the sky, not like a caterpillar turning into a butterfly."[3]

3. Transcendence or the Absolute (conscious consciousness)

Ken Wilber has already responded in the previous chapter to the paradoxical notion that there is a need for process and no need for process in attaining P-A. He continues with that theme here: "This radical realization, existing in the timeless and ever present moment, can occur at virtually any stage of development and is *not* the result of any cause, because it is itself timeless and ever present, uncaused and unborn. Nonetheless, there is abundant cross-cultural evidence that the higher one's degree of consciousness development, the *more likely* this realization can occur.... Enlightenment is not the highest stage of temporal development, but a stepping off of the cycle of temporal development altogether."

The Now is always present and has no cause, yet Wilber says that "...consciousness development can make it more likely to be realized..." and he says that "[I] talk about getting out of development entirely and recognizing the ever present One Taste."[4] In the same letter Wilber quotes the Zen master Ma Tsu: "If there is any development in the Tao, the completion of that development is really the ruin and destruction of the Tao. But if there is no development at all, one remains completely unenlightened."[5]

C. G. Jung gives us the perspective of Jungian psychology as it relates to transcendence. "Transcendent function ... arises from the union of the conscious and the unconscious attitudes.... There are several sources for this unconscious material, the most useful for the constructive method of therapy being spontaneous fantasies [creating in the present moment]. The patient must give himself over to his mood and give form to his fantasies and other associations by writing, visualizing, or some form of artwork.... The opposite ego and the unconscious must be reconciled in order to bring about the transcendent function.... The value of this transcendent function derives from the fact that it provides a way for the patient to break the dependence on the therapist and to attain liberation by his own efforts [self-reliance]."[6]

Jane Roberts in her book *The Nature of Personal Reality*, "channels" Seth who always has an interesting perspective when given challenging questions. About the nature of the state of grace, truer words were never spoken. "The state of grace is a condition in which all growth is effortless, a transparent, joyful acquiescence that is a ground requirement of all existence. Your own body grows naturally and easily from its time of birth, not expecting resistance but taking its miraculous unfolding for granted; using all of itself with great, gracious, creatively aggressive abandon.

"You were born into a state of grace, therefore. It is impossible for you to leave it. You will die in a state of grace whether or not special words are spoken for you, or water or oil is poured over your head. You share this blessing with the animals and all other living things. You cannot 'fall out of' grace, nor can it be taken from you.

"You *can* ignore it [as we do in P-B]. You can hold beliefs that blind you to its existence. You will still be graced but unable to perceive your own uniqueness and integrity, and blind also to other attributes with which you are automatically gifted."[7]

Returning to Hinduism as a source for the principles of transcendence we start with the necessity of transcending the ego and any thought of "I" or "me." "It is *Sat-Chit-Ananda* (Being-Consciousness-Bliss) in which there is not even the slightest trace of the 'I' thought. This is also called *Mouna* (Silence) or *Atma* (Self). That is the only thing that is."[8]

Fritjof Capra in his book, *The Tao of Physics,* adds both Hindu and Buddhist viewpoints on transcendence. "The Upanishads, for example, speak about a higher and lower knowledge and associate the lower knowledge with various sciences, the higher with religious awareness. Buddhists talk about 'relative' and 'absolute' knowledge or about 'conditional truth' and 'transcendental truth.'"[9]

The struggle between our desire to transcend the nightmare of P-B and our fear of doing so meet in the present moment and provide us a choice to react or respond. I think that Jon Kabat-Zinn was speaking of the survival strategy of the false self when he wrote: "At some level, people know they have elaborate patterns to keep themselves as far away from that deep experience as possible."[10] Seth refers to a profound response, such as our Point of Power Practice, and the process of reconditioning or behavior modification which can change our reactions into responses, fear into compassion. "Your desire or belief will literally be reaching back into time, teaching the nerves new tricks. Definite reorganizations in that past will occur in your present, allowing you to behave in entirely new fashions."[11]

We have come full circle in this chapter as we return to the perfection of the present moment. Sakyuong Mipham Rinpoche, the son of the important Buddhist teacher and founder of Naropa University,

Trungpa Rinpoche, completes our exploration of transcendence. "We are saying that perfectly endowed, complete enlightenment begins with our motivation to regard everything we experience right now—and the whole world—as perfect and pristine. We call this the motivation of great purity and great equality. As Vajrayana practitioners, we are asked to develop the motivation to wake up and see ourselves and the world as we truly are."[12]

We are being asked to stop making transcendence complicated, difficult and remote. We are being asked to embrace Simple Reality.

Chapter Nineteen

Fear

Human Energy Has Been Used To Create A Fear-Driven Narrative But We Can Always Use That Energy To Express A Story Wherein Compassion Is The Dominant Human Expression

Human energy, the motive power of the life we have been given, is neutral and is accompanied by free will which is also a wonderful gift of life. How we use these gifts when deciding how we want to live on this planet makes all the difference in what our experience has been and will be. Understanding the part played by fear in creating an unsustainable human community will help us make better choices in the future.

> *And if it is a fear you would dispel, the seat of that fear is in your heart and not in the hand of the feared.*
> Kahlil Gibran[1]

The perfect beginning for this article is Einstein's crucial question that we have used before. Is the universe friendly or not? To answer in the negative reveals our containment in P-B. In working with his clients, therapist Philip Kavanaugh, affirms the importance of Einstein's insight. "The panic attacks, anxiety, and depressions that I have observed are all symptoms resulting from a feeling of being alone and helpless in an uncaring universe."[2] Fear is inescapable without the ability to enter the present moment by ceasing our reactive behaviors.

> *Fear of death was the first thing on earth to make the gods.*
> Lucretius[3]

Religion as Lucretius realized was born out of fear which tells us that conventional religion and P-A are incompatible. However, Edward Edinger realized that in P-B both believers and unbelievers alike cannot escape fear. "If one is a religious believer he will be afraid of acknowledging his unconscious doubt. If one has no religious beliefs, he will be afraid to admit his sense of spiritual emptiness."[4]

> *Nothing real can be threatened.*
> *Nothing unreal exists.*
> *Herein lies the peace of God.*
>   *A Course in Miracles*

A Course in Miracles transcends conventional religious beliefs, attitudes and values and is a good source of P-A principles, including the absence of fear. Responding or fearlessness is nothing more than being in the Now. We can never repeat too often the observation of the great teacher J. Krishnamurti when he was asked to give the reason for his fearless state of being. "I don't mind what's happening," he said, and he meant that he was not reacting to life out of fear. We can see the relationship between fear and the false-self energy centers when we create suffering by seeking to satisfy our basic need for security, sensation and power. Only in P-A can we profoundly understand what the words from *A Course in Miracles* or Krishnamurti's words really mean and which human behaviors are truly "fearless."

A "circle of fear" is a closed loop which is difficult to break out of without a shift in worldview from P-B to P-A. Unconsciousness (lack of awareness) = resistance to reality = fear = afflictive emotions = addictive (habitual) reactions related to security, sensation and power (the false-self energy centers) = unconsciousness. Hence, around and around we go ad infinitum. As we shift toward right view or awareness of the nature of reality (P-A), we begin to spiral upward toward increased consciousness. Or we can "shift" immediately into the NOW beyond reaction into compassionate awareness. When this happens there is no evolution or process or circular movement only the serenity, peace and joy of being in the present moment.

In her exposition of *A Course in Miracles* entitled *A Return to Love,* Marianne Williamson expresses a realization that she feels we would all do well to internalize: "Fear is the root of all evil. It's the problem with the world."[5] Again, from *A Course in Miracle* answering the question: What if I don't want to give up my fears because they help me protect myself? "What you give up is merely the illusion of protecting illusions. And it is this you fear, and only this. How foolish to be afraid of nothing!...Your defenses will not work, but you are not in danger. Recognize this, and they will disappear. And only then will you accept your real protection."[6] A good acronym is FEAR (False Evidence Appearing Real).

Eckhart Tolle, the author of *The Power of Now*, relates fear to Oneness. "Internal and external are ultimately one. When you no longer perceive the world as hostile, there is no more fear, and when there is no more fear, you think, speak and act differently. Love and compassion arise, and they affect the world."[7]

Notice how fear is related to the inability to give a profound response to two of the Great Questions. Rollo May realized this when he concluded that: "This bewilderment—this confusion as to who we are and what we should do—is the most painful thing about anxiety."[8] To dispel fear it is crucial that we have a profound response to the Three Great Questions (first introduced in Chapter 1). Internalizing P-A will give us those answers. Then we will have an identity that will make us at home in the universe, unlike Willy Loman.

> *He never knew who he was.*
> Arthur Miller from *Death of a Salesman*

Fear is unavoidable for the newborn infant who is dependent upon others as he/she begins to develop the survival strategy that will later have to be transcended to overcome fear-driven reactions. Dr. William Gaylin in *Adam and Eve and Pinnochio: On Becoming Human,* confirms this early challenge as a source of fear. "This rapid early development will lead the neonate to the crucial inference that is the primary lesson of infancy: survival depends on the beneficence of some protective others, not yet identified as parents. Terror, therefore, is equated with abandonment, separation, or even simple isolation. Separation anxiety is the model on which all later insecurities will be elaborated."[9]

Philip Kavanaugh learned in his counseling practice that in constructing the sensation portion of our survival strategy, which results in our addictive behaviors, fear plays a crucial role. "It is important to recognize that fear is the hallmark of all unhealthy addictions, addictions which block us from looking within or listening to our intuition and feelings. It is fear that keeps us from finding inner spiritual wisdom—the kind of discernment and insight which are our healing source."[10]

How can we explain why so few people are able to awaken into the present moment? Could it be fear? And if so, what is the basis of that fear? Ontology, the branch of philosophy that deals with "being" may have our answer. From Rollo May's book *The Discovery of Being* we have: "Anxiety is *the experience of the threat of imminent nonbeing.*"[11] It seems we have anxiety if we believe in the ultimate reality of death or nonbeing. In P-A, we know better than that because we do not identify with the body and are free from existential anxiety. If however, humanity continues to ignore its suffering, we may expect to experience more of that guilt, shame, regret and anxiety that characterizes our life in P-B.

The importance of facing our fear in the present moment and choosing response over reaction is critically important. The alternatives are, as we know, unacceptable. Using the terminology of the existentialists we have three choices. First, we must summon what Paul Tillich called "the courage to be" and face our anxiety on the way to "being" or P-A. Secondly, if we choose reaction we will experience guilt at having missed our only opportunity to achieve Self-realization. And, finally if we submit to fear, we will also experience ennui, the boredom and self-loathing that results from believing that we have done nothing and have become nothing. In the existential choice of being and nothingness, we will have chosen the nothingness of P-B.

"The illusory foundation of our normal outlook, said Gandhi, is fear. But fear has no place in our hearts once we have eradicated the most ingrained attachments, particularly those involving wealth, pleasure and safety [security, sensation and power]. Gandhi also said that we become intrepid when we no longer consider ourselves owners, but 'trustees' of what life has assigned to us, and no longer masters making demands on others, but servants who have nothing to lose. Then 'all fears will roll away like mists.'"[12]

There is no fear in love; but perfect love drives out fear.
I John 4:18

The mystic and former Catholic priest, Matthew Fox sees "that ole time religion" as a source of fear. "A devastating psychological corollary of the fall/redemption tradition is that religion with original sin as its starting point and religion built exclusively around sin and redemption does not teach trust. Such religion does not teach trust of existence or of body or of society or of creativity or of cosmos. [It does not teach that the universe is friendly.] It teaches both consciously and unconsciously, verbally and non-verbally, *fear.*"[13]

Fear is the absence of compassion just as darkness, which has no substantial reality, is the absence of light. The religious concept of redemption then is not the overcoming of sin, which has no substantial reality, but in the overcoming of fear. Thomas Troward focuses on the role that the mind plays in creating fear. "'We are surrounded by all sorts of circumstances that we do not desire.' Yes, you *fear* them, and in so doing you *think* them; and in this way you are constantly exercising this Divine prerogative of creation by Thought, only through ignorance you use it in a wrong direction."[14]

Why doesn't our political system, our government, seem to be able to identify and solve problems? Could it be that it is a fear-driven institution? In the 1992 presidential election James Squires, Ross Perot's top media adviser gives us the answer. "The whole thing in politics is fear. We always vote for who we are most comfortable with," Squires said. "So you try to make the world afraid."[15]

The people I am scared of are the people who are scared.
Robert Frost

As we shift from P-B to P-A, we begin eliminating the experience of the energy of fear. The Point of Power Practice enables us to begin to reduce the level of fear and replace it with the energy of compassion. The absence of fear (the realization of Oneness) makes possible the full experience of the present moment, the full experience of Simple Reality. This is the highest human attainment—this is why we are here on this planet—in this place at this time.

Fear is excitement without the breath.
Fritz Perls

Building on Perls' observation we can add that fear is energy that presents us with an opportunity to choose a response or a reaction. If we choose to identify with the mind, body or emotions then we will react and that energy will become an afflictive emotion in P-B. If we employ the Point of Power Practice, breathe and respond, then the energy becomes compassion and is contained in the eternal Now of P-A and we will have transcended fear. And each time that we do this, fear, like all other illusions will lose its energy and fade away like a summer mirage on the blinding-hot interstate.

Chapter Twenty

Compassion

The Most Fundamental And Authentic Human Behavior Is That Of Compassion

The relationship between compassion and fear will help us understand why we have made poor choices in the past in creating our human community. We have now reached the point where we can begin making different choices more in harmony with our true self, our essence, as human beings. It is time to deny the false self the energy it needs to control our behavior and begin to support the true self and its natural emergence as the only true reality, our true identity.

> *You may call God love, you may call God goodness. But the best name for God is compassion.*
> Meister Eckhart

Compassion is the ultimate outcome of the Point of Power Practice, the result of entering P-A. Fear is the fundamental cause of unconsciousness because any movement toward consciousness, toward Simple Reality, is blocked by fear until we find a way to move past that fear. Simple Reality provides us the means to do that. Compassion and fear can be thought of as being on a continuum with one's position determined by relative awareness, i.e. having little awareness results in more fear and less compassion and, conversely, having greater awareness results in more compassion and less fear.

In *The Nature of Personal Reality,* Seth has profound insights that contrast paradigms A and B. "It is often said that man believes in devils because he believes in gods. The fact is that man began to believe in demons when he started to feel a sense of guilt. The guilt itself arose with the birth of compassion. Animals have a sense of justice that you do not understand, and built-in to that innocent sense of integrity there is a biological compassion, understood at the deepest cellular levels. In your terms man is an animal, rising out of himself, from himself evolving *certain* animal capacities to their utmost; not forming new physical specializations of body any longer..., but creating from his needs [false self survival strategy], desires .... To varying degrees this same impetus resides throughout all creaturehood."[1]

How did humans then evolve from operating according to instinct to behaving according to volition? In other words, how did we develop the need for a survival strategy? "Such a task meant that man must break out of the self-regulating, precise, safe and yet limiting aspects of instinct. The birth of a conscious mind, as you think of it, meant that the species took upon itself free will. Built-in procedures that had beautifully sufficed could now be superseded. They became suggestions instead of rules. Compassion 'rose' [arose] from the biological structure up to emotional reality. The 'new' consciousness accepted its emerging reality. The 'new' consciousness accepted its emerging triumph—freedom—and was faced with responsibility for action of a conscious level, and with the birth of guilt."[2]

> *The cat eats the mouse.*
> *Neither exist.*
> *Do not tell them.*
> Anonymous haiku

Of course there was a "cost" to the loss of instinctive innocence and that was a loss of the sense of Oneness that we now have the opportunity to regain but this time at a conscious level. "At certain levels both cat and mouse understands the nature of the life energy they share, and are not—in those terms—jealous for their own individuality. This does not mean they will not struggle to live, but that they have a built-in unconscious sense of unity with nature in *which they know they will not be lost or immersed*. Man, pursuing his own way, chose to step outside of that framework—on a conscious level. The birth of compassion then took the place of the animals' innate knowledge; the biological compassion turned into emotional realization."[3]   That "emotional realization" is what I have labeled "feeling" in this book.

"Joseph Campbell," writes Joan Borysenko, "calls compassion the flower of psychospiritual growth."[4]   We have the opportunity in P-A to identify with the suffering in the world and our own suffering, not as a personal pain but as a suffering that unites all of humanity. *This* is compassion and it is healing for us personally and for humanity collectively as our increasing ability to respond compassionately creates an awareness of Simple Reality and delivers us into the present moment.

Chapter Twenty One

The Implicate Order

What Is The Source Of Wisdom And Energy Which Connects All Of Creation And How Can We Use It?

The implicate order is the keystone that directs the energies of the overarching narrative of Simple Reality and sustains the structure of P-A. If the implicate order is so foundational to the human story, why isn't it taught in high school physics and psychology or why isn't it basic to the teachings of religious mythology? Good question!

We will discover that divergent thinkers in the realm of physics acknowledge the implicate order. In describing what has been called by Maslow a "peak experience" and by others the Akashic record, the implicate order or simply "the field," the scientist Ervin Laszlo in his book *Quantum Shift in the Global Brain: How the New Scientific Reality Can Change Us and our World, says:* "'It is the confirmation of something people have always felt but could not give a rational explanation for; our close connection to each other and to the cosmos.'" Robert Smith continues this idea in his article "Science discovers the Akashic field." "Hindu sages intuitively knew about the existence of what they labeled in ancient Sanskrit—*Akasha.* [*Akashic* originally meant space, ether or sky.] The Hindu seers were on the right track…. There is a deeper reality in the cosmos, a reality that is an Akashic field that connects and creates coherence."[1]

Glenn Parry explains why we often ignore our intuitional promptings. "One reason we do not generally recognize the primacy of the implicate order is that we have become so habituated to the explicate order and emphasized it so much in our *thought and language* [italics mine] that we tend strongly to feel that our primary experience is of that which is explicate and manifest."[2]

As always the problem is our focus on the outer world of form in P-B which gives the intellect dominance over our intuition – our guide in P-A. Those scientists who trust their inner wisdom as did Einstein and Ervin Laszlo in his book entitled *Science and the Reenchantment of the Cosmos: The Rise of the Integral Vision of Reality* have the advantage of seeing more deeply into the nature of reality as it really is. "Scientific data here have stimulated Laszlo to suggest that there is a deep field of information, which he calls the 'Akashic Field' or 'A-field' that bonds the interrelated parts of the universe."[3]

Christian DeQuincy relates how physicists have discovered a universal information field and have called it the zero point energy field—the ZPE field. "ZPE theory explains how the world we know and live in—our undeniable, familiar reality—springs forth billions of times a second from the universal field of quantum potential. Everything we know, everything that exists, comes from the ZPE field, and sooner or later returns there—to be 'recycled' back into the world in some form, or perhaps into another universe."[4]

The theory of English physicist David Bohm, a colleague of Einstein, suggests that the information of the entire universe is contained in each of its parts. "Ken Wilber summarizes Bohm's theory in *The Holographic Paradigm:* 'In Bohm's terminology, under the *explicate realm* of separate things and events is an *implicate realm* of undivided wholeness, and this implicate whole is simultaneously available to each explicate part. In other words, the physical universe itself seems to be a gigantic hologram, with each part being in the whole and the whole being in each part."[5]

Will Keepin continues fleshing out Bohm's postulate. "So Bohm proposes a tripartite structure to reality: matter, energy, and meaning. Moreover, each of these basic notions enfolds the other two. Thus, 'energy' consists not only of explicate energy, but also includes implicate matter and implicate meaning. Put another way, energy 'enfolds' both matter and meaning. Similarly, matter enfolds energy and meaning. And finally, meaning enfolds both matter and energy.... Meaning lives in the implicate order and is just as real as matter and energy.[6] Notice how Keepin's following description of the implicate order might just as well be called "Oneness" or Simple Reality. "So for Bohm, the nature of the cosmos is a single, unitive process—an unbroken, flowing wholeness in which each part of the flow contains the entire flow."[7]

We don't directly perceive the implicate order but can "feel" it during sitting meditation and other contemplative forms of practice or during the "flow" of the creative process. Keepin's continued description explains why most of us are unfamiliar with concepts such as Oneness or the implicate order. "The cosmos is a single, unbroken wholeness in flowing movement.... Furthermore, Bohm proposed that there are two fundamental aspects to the holomovement: the *explicate order* and the *implicate order*. ...the explicate and implicate order only *appear* as distinct—although convincingly so—because of our perceptual limitations. That which we don't directly see, hear, taste, feel, touch, or think—constitutes the implicate order. Thus Bohm posits a vast realm called the 'implicate order' that lies beyond what we directly perceive in the physical universe. The implicate order is beyond space and time altogether, although it's accessible at every point in space-time. It's present everywhere, but visible nowhere."[8]

We can also find psychologists who acknowledge the existence of the implicate order. The most intuitive psychologists have observed that humanity has a reciprocal relationship with the implicate order – we draw from it and contribute to it. "Jung...concluded that the individual unconscious could draw on the deeper pool of the collective unconscious and find correspondences at the mythic level of which a patient might be totally unaware."[9]

The implicate order is also accessible in dreams as Jung discovered in working with his patients and in his research. Whether in dreams or as conscious inspiration, artists draw on the implicate order to create beauty. Jung gives the example of a dream that R. L. Stevenson had: "The British author Robert Louis Stevenson had spent years looking for a story that would fit his 'strong sense of man's double being,' when the plot of *Dr. Jekyll and Mr. Hyde* was suddenly revealed to him in a dream."[10] In Stevenson's "double being" we recognize the true-self and false-self aspects of human behavior.

Since human intuition is universal and not bound by time we can expect that awareness of the implicate order goes back to the beginning of civilization. We turn to Marcus Aurelius speaking about what he intuits will happen after death, "Every part of me then will be reduced by change into some part of the universe, and that again will change into another part of the universe, and so on forever."[11]

The Roman emperor would have made a good quantum physicist considering the way he understood indestructible energy. "The universal nature out of the universal substance [energy], as if it were wax, now moulds a horse, and when it has broken this up, it uses the material for a tree, then for a man, then for something else; and each of these things subsists for a very short time. But it is no hardship for the vessel to be broken up, just as there was none in its being fastened together."[12]

Continuing to listen to mystics both incarnate and the "dis-incarnate" we turn to the American mystic/philosopher Ralph Waldo Emerson who spoke of the implicate order in the language of those who "see" beyond the material world. "The truth is in the air, and the most impressionable brain will announce it first...."[13] In other words, we are immersed in the implicate order as a fish is immersed in the ocean. Continuing to deny that we are a fish and that there is no ocean will only lead to difficulty in surviving in our environment.

Thanks to the extensive notes kept by her husband Rob and to Jane Roberts' "Seth books," we can experience their weekly sessions in upstate New York where Jane channeled a very profound intelligence Seth. Seth explains how the creative process and problem solving works in the context of the implicate order. "Your cells' multidimensional knowledge is usually not consciously available, nor can they put it into psychological terms for you. Such work with the imagination acts as a trigger, however, drawing information to you from other levels of your greater reality, and concentrating it on the specific problem at hand. It will then appear in terms understandable to your own experience."[14]

Seth is saying that our thoughts are also tangible energy, " In what may seem to you to be an odd analogy I will compare your thoughts with viruses, for they are alive, always present, responsive, and possess their own kind of mobility. Physically speaking at least, thoughts are chemically propelled, and they travel through the universal body as viruses travel through your temporal form."[15]

The English mystic, Judge Thomas Troward, adds another all-important characteristic of the implicate order, namely, the infinite potential for creation that it gives each one of us. "…all Nature is pervaded by an interior personalness, infinite in its potentialities of intelligence, responsiveness, and power of expression, and only waiting to be called into activity by our recognition of it."[16] As Troward implies, it is imperative that we recognize our power to change our experience of the human condition.

Troward, a Christian, also found the implicate order and the creative process implicit in the Bible. "Involution, the passing of Spirit into Form is antecedent to the passing of Form into Consciousness. …[and] Spirit's ONE mode of action, which is Thought, are the basis of all that the Bible has to teach us, and therefore from its first page to its last, we shall find these two ideas continually recurring in a variety of different connections, the ONE-ness of the Divine Spirit and the Creative Power of Man's Thought, which the Bible expresses in its two grand statements, that 'God is ONE,' and that Man is made 'in the image and likeness of God.' These are the two fundamental statements of the Bible, and all its other statements flow logically from them…."[17] Oneness and perfection define Simple Reality.

Rocco Errico, gives us the perspective of the Middle Eastern region where early Christianity was more deeply connected to the implicate order than it is today. "Easterners often say, 'Our senses are capable of hearing the intimate whisperings of the divine Spirit.' Over forty percent of the Bible is based on mysticism. The spectrum of mysticism encompasses dreams, visions, voices, healings, clairaudience (inner hearing), clairvoyance (inner sight), and bi-location (out of body experiences)."[18]

Being in the present moment and connected to the implicate order is our natural state which is why children demonstrate an amazing "presence" before they "fall" into unconsciousness as a result of constructing their survival strategy. Matthew Fox, a Christian mystic, offers the following stories which illustrate this point. "…I received a letter from a five-year-old child. He tells me that 'there are four kinds of beans—green beans, pork and beans, jelly beans, and human beings. Human beings are special.' 'Why are human beings special?' he was asked. He replied, 'People eat green beans, jelly beans, and pork and beans and God eats human beings. God likes us and eats us. We become part of God and live in God's belly all our life…. God's belly is the whole earth.' Where did you get these ideas?' he was asked. 'From inside myself,' he replied.

Fox gives us a second priceless example of the wisdom of children before they lose their connection to the implicate order. "In a kindergarten class in Colorado, children were asked to draw a picture of Jesus. They all obliged but only one six-year-old girl drew a picture different from the bearded figure all the other students drew. She drew a picture of herself."[19]

The American mystic, Ernest Holmes, author of *The Science of Mind* (a New Thought text), affirms the power of human thought within the paradigm of Simple Reality and does so with an analogy of how the Akashic field or implicate order actually work. "Let us find an example in electricity. It *is*. It has no goals. But it can be individualized into light, heat or power. We can say, however, that the Universal Undifferentiated Intelligence contains a quality of being or consciousness which is capable of responding to each of us in the terms of our own approach to It. It, therefore, reflects wisdom to the thinker, peace to the peaceful and love to the lover."[20] This explains why in P-B we are creating so many experiences that reflect human fear rather than beauty and compassion.

Holmes continues labeling the implicate order "Subjective Mind." "Subjective Mind being Universal, the history of the race is written in the mental atmosphere of the globe on which we live. That is, everything which has ever happened on this planet has left its imprint on the walls of time; and could we walk down their corridors and read the writings, we should be reading the race history... There is a tendency, on the part of all of us, to reproduce the accumulated subjective experiences of the human race."[21]   C. G. Jung would recognize this as the description of what he called the "collective unconscious." Ironically, we can use the power of the implicate order to transcend the influence of the collective unconscious and the self-destructive behavior of the survival strategy of the false self. Now we can begin to see the importance of acknowledging the reality of the implicate order.

The universality of the implicate order is also obvious when we encounter it in the sacred texts of the Hindu/Buddhist tradition. Modern Hindu and Buddhist writers and practitioners continue to reinforce the all-important principle that we create our own reality.

The implicate order as energy and only energy has been described by physicists as a "field" or "fields," a term used by Deepak Chopra in describing subatomic particles. "These particles aren't material objects but fluctuating fields of energy in a larger, universal field of energy. However, as long as we are stuck in a perceptual mode, we only see that limited world-view."[22]   Chopra helps us get a sense that the dominant (P-B) worldview is highly egocentric, relative and clueless as to the nature of reality. "The eye of the honeybee only sees honey at a distance because its eye cells are not sensitive to the usual [human] range of colors. A snake senses its environment through infrared radiation. A bat senses its whole universe through sonar. What's the real picture of the world? There isn't such a thing. In order to go beyond this perceptual artifact called "reality" we have to make an inner journey. That can only come by transcending the senses..." And that can only come by detaching our identity from the body, mind and emotions until our entire life becomes a focused meditation responding to a deeper reality, that is to say, by responding to Simple Reality.

Another way to think about ultimate reality is to characterize it as one Mind as do the advocates of New Thought. Deepak Chopra does not see this as different from the concept of the implicate order. "We believe that this unified field is one of intelligence and that mind is not confined to the brain, nor even to the body. It pervades the entire cosmos. Our brains merely structure our thought processes, which represent limited aspects of a more universal mind."[23]

Hearing from the Buddhist teacher who had the greatest influence on American Buddhists in recent times, we see that the Buddhist worldview acknowledges how we can use the implicate order to experience Simple Reality. The founder of Naropa University in Boulder, Chogyam Trungpa Rinpoche, continues to encourage humanity to adopt a more profound worldview. "You actually can connect your own intrinsic wisdom with a sense of greater wisdom or vision beyond you. You might think that something extraordinary will happen to you when you discover magic. Something extraordinary does happen. You simply find yourself in the realm of utter reality, complete and thorough reality."[24]

As we peel away the layers of illusion, choosing response again and again instead of reacting, we reveal our natural state. Connecting to the implicate order in this way we experience a joy-filled life, we find ourselves in the numinous kingdom of Simple Reality.

Chapter Twenty Two

The Algebra Of Simple Reality

Mystics Have Been Very Creative In Teaching Simple Reality

"Like the other teachers of his time, Buddha taught through conversation, lectures, and parables. Since it never occurred to him, any more than to Socrates or Christ, to put his doctrine into writing, he summarized it in *sutras* ("threads") designed to prompt the memory…. His discourses took the form of Socratic questioning, moral parables, courteous controversy, or succinct formulas whereby he sought to compress his teaching into convenient brevity and order."[1] Buddha understood that Simple Reality is indeed simple.

Like all great teachers, Buddha also added humor to simplicity to reach even the most resistant student. "Like Lao-tze and Christ he wished to return good for evil, love for hate; and he remained silent under misunderstanding and abuse. 'If a man foolishly does me wrong, I will return to him the protection of my ungrudging love; the more evil comes from him, the more good shall come from me.' When a simpleton abused him, Buddha listened in silence; but when the man had finished, Buddha asked him: 'Son, if a man declined to accept a present made to him, to whom would it belong?' The man answered: 'To him who offered it.' 'My son,' said Buddha, 'I decline to accept your abuse, and request you to keep it for yourself.'"[2]

As mystics (when experiencing the present moment) we have the opportunity to become creative teachers by passing along the principles of Simple Reality. For example, as perfect creations within a perfect creation, we surely regard the notion of sin as absurd. It is indeed nonsensical as is this easy-to-remember acronym suggests.

S I N = Self-Imposed Nonsense

The principles of P-A are few in number, simple of course, but also formulaic, that is, they can be expressed in algebraic terms. For example, the formula S+S+S = S. This formula relates to the need to have a foundation or context that supports transcendence, insight or "the shift." Without Simplicity, Silence, or Solitude, we will find it hard to experience Serenity. In other words, response will be difficult and we will be more likely to react because we will be agitated and distracted from the reality of our deeper more serene nature. Being too wrapped up in the noise, complexity and competition of P-B we will persist, in spite of ourselves, to create personal suffering by continually reacting.

S + S + S = S
Simplicity + Silence + Solitude = Serenity

S+R = S is the second formula and means Stimulus (trigger) plus Reaction = Suffering. All human suffering is caused by wanting things to be different and reacting when it isn't what we think it "should" be. We have a moment between the trigger, that is when something we don't like happens in our environment, and when we choose to react rather than choosing to respond. Now we can change R in the formula by choosing Response instead of Reaction and thereby change the outcome from Suffering to Freedom. (S+R = F), freedom from suffering, that is. That moment of choice is the "point" in the Point of Power Practice. That is when we take time to relax, breathe and refuse to identify with the body, mind or emotions and remain in the present moment.

S + R = S
Stimulus + Reaction = Suffering

S + R = S
Stimulus + Response = Serenity

We have Brugh Joy to thank for this formula for happiness. This wonderful formula reveals common false-self behaviors which lead to suffering.

    A + B + C = H
        A Don't judge
        B Don't compare
        C Release the need to know why
        H Happiness

In his autobiography Han Shan, the Chinese Zen master, remembers one of his dreams: "…he met Maitreya, the future Buddha, who told him that wisdom is to be found in not making divisions and comparisons."[3]

Piero Ferrucci, in his book *Inevitable Grace,* writes, "…I am conscious [present] while …brushing my teeth…But then I am distracted, and my consciousness is a thousand miles away; I judge, and thereby separate myself from reality; I compare the present situation with a past one, and immediately feel divided within; I start daydreaming, and already I am asleep, absent, carried off to another world."[4] That other world is P-B and our habits are deeply conditioned in order to survive in that paradigm.

From Nisargadatta Maharaj and his book *I Am That,* comes the formula KN+HN+DN=H. This is one of the most radical, profound and challenging of the formulas in our P-A algebra. Know Nothing plus Have Nothing plus Do Nothing are behavioral guides to Happiness. This is the classic negative, (i.e. what *not to do)* Eastern approach to attaining P-A.

    KN + HN + DN = H
    Know Nothing + Have Nothing + Do Nothing = Happiness

The intellect or "knowing" will not get us to Nirvana. Accumulation of material wealth or "having" is pointless. And assiduous "effort" or "doing" as the Buddha discovered after six years of ascetic practice was also futile. We cannot *attain* happiness, we *are* happiness.

Work with these formulae everyday and you will find that the algebra of Simple Reality will aid you in the process of reconditioning your reactive behavior. These new behaviors are the foundation for making our moment-to-moment life a meditation that will lead to an experience of Simple Reality, a shift to P-A.

Chapter Twenty Three

Right View

Experiencing Oneness, The Inter-Connection And Inter-Relatedness Of All Of Creation, Influences All Of Us To Treat Each Other And The Environment With Compassion

Most practitioners of meditation understand that the goal of their practice is to experience "reality" or what we call Simple Reality. To understand what that experience is or will be requires an understanding of what Buddhists call "right view," which is one of the precepts in the Buddha's Eightfold Path. Before starting out on a journey it is only prudent to know where we are going. The map called Simple Reality has on it a highway labeled "via Right View." This is the route that leads to where we want to go.

In the process of attaining an experience of Simple Reality what is the significance of right view? "While belief per se tends not to be a central concern for Buddhists, how we see the world—what is sometimes known as 'the view'—is. How we see the world determines how we will act within it."[1]   That explanation by Barry Boyce is a good starting point for this chapter because changing our behavior is all-important.

The capacity to discern the true nature of a situation, to penetrate to the essence, to the reality of our experience, is empowered by a profound perspective, by a right view. To wake up we must become observers of our own personal experience. Through that process of observation we will gain profound insights into the nature of reality. These breakthroughs are at the heart of shifting from the relative to the Absolute and the attainment of what the Buddha called right view. Through right view we arrive into the present moment, the Now. We arrive at the place that we never left and experience it for the first time.

The consequences of experiencing life from the perspective of an illusory paradigm, as most of us know, results in a life of suffering and is, "... the experience [that] confused beings develop as a result of unawareness, and instead of the five modes of knowledge, the five poisons, or emotional afflictions, arise. The dualistic sense of self and other is born, and the illusory self gradually perceives the external world as filled with the objects of its desire, hatred, pride, envy and delusion. In this way, existence in the six realms of *samsara* [suffering] comes about, entirely based on mistaken perception."[2] In Buddhist language, Francesca Freemantle has expressed very clearly the importance of right view.

Right view can also come as a sudden insight, as a spontaneous paradigm shift. The Buddha spoke of right view "with taints" and right view "without taints." The Hindu *Bhagavata Purana VI* describes those two states. "Soon his mind was illumined, and he had the vision of the God of Love. He felt overwhelming joy in his heart, and attained peace and tranquility. As he continued his practices there came greater and greater illumination, and he ultimately realized his unity with Brahman."[3] So must we also "continue our practice" (response "without taints") gradually increasing our ratio of responses to reactions by means of the Point of Power Practice.

"In this book [*The Nature of Personal Reality*], Seth is saying that you can change your experience by altering your beliefs about yourself and physical existence.... Seth's main idea is that we create our personal reality through our conscious beliefs about ourselves, others, and the world. Following this is the concept that the 'point of power' is in the present, not in the past of this life or any other."[4] "You get what you concentrate upon."[5] And what we must concentrate upon is Simple Reality.

The Buddha saw the attainment of right view as a two-step process in which he felt that the precepts of the Eightfold Path had to be observed first. He explained that first one has right view, but that this is initial insight, not free from "taints." Therefore one sets about establishing morality much as a Christian would be expected to observe the Ten Commandments. With continued progress, one learns how to purify the mind, making it then possible to have Wisdom, and therefore, right view "free from taints." The first set of obstacles is cognitive or intellectual in nature, what could be called core beliefs. A paradigm shift involving the attainment of right view will change our fundamental understanding of these "taints." Then we must employ the Point of Power Practice to work on the deeper conditioning and over time we will arrive at the insight "free from taints" or reactions.

As we have said many times, the principles of Simple Reality must be repeated over and over again because we are involved in reconditioning our deeply ingrained behavior patterns. So we have established that what is needed then is a paradigm shift. The reason we need a paradigm shift is that most other attempts to address human suffering address only symptoms and not the causes. Without a paradigm shift, we are wasting our time although it may seem otherwise. For example, the widow of MLK Jr., Coretta Scott King, laments that "One of the failings of the [Civil Rights] Movement was that, while we taught people to fight against the system, and how to respect themselves, we didn't teach young people that they would have to fight all over again."[6]   So without a paradigm shift, without a change to right view, we cannot make lasting or profound change.

As we have learned in other chapters in this book, a paradigm shift will drive a shift in identity. The following quote from the Zen practitioner Master Sheng-Yen describes an intellectual understanding of what the new identity is occasioned by a shift in worldview. "The second way to transcend the ego is the conceptual way. It happens when there's a sudden and complete change in one's viewpoint. It can happen for example, when one's reading a *sutra* or listening to a dharma talk. In an instant, one can become enlightened. But for this to really work, a person has to already want to know the answer to the question, 'What is the ego, what is the self?'"[7]   It is also effective in shifting identity to forget about the ego and learn what the true self is *not*. The true self is not the body, mind or emotions.

Here is a description of what right view is *not* from Vedanta (non-dualistic) Hinduism. "Thus the memory, which has attained to the level of direct perception, is spoken of in the *Shruti* [scripture] as a means of liberation. 'This Atman [true self] is not to be reached through various sciences, nor by intellect, nor by much study of the Vedas. Whomsoever this Atman desires, by him is the Atman attained; unto him this Atman reveals himself.' Hereafter saying that mere hearing, thinking, and meditating are not the means of attaining this Atman..."[8]

Many Hindus also understood the importance of distinguishing Simple Reality (right view) from P-B. "In order to escape *samsara* (the cycle of birth and death), we must free ourselves from the desire for phenomenal things by discriminating between the Real and the unreal."[9] In fact there was much agreement in Hindu/Buddhist scripture that the shift to right view was a prerequisite for entering the present moment. "In this connection, the sages have spoken of ... qualifications for attainment....First is mentioned discrimination between the eternal and the non-eternal [P-A and P-B]."[10] In the words of Vivekananda: "Only those can understand who have perceived the Reality."[11]

Ken Wilber in a conversation with Andrew Cohen hints at the importance of a day-to-day continuous use of the Point of Power Practice after a profound insight has occurred. "What's so interesting to me is that both top-down [right-view realization] and bottom up [evolution of consciousness through practice] have a role to play. That awakening event—when a person *acknowledges* that the already liberated self is something that is in the fabric of their awareness that they had simply not noticed—*is* profound transformation. But then the person comes out of that state. And, as you say, there's the whole process of how much does it stick, can they align themselves with it."[12] If one has a profound context or worldview combined with a profound practice, the transformation will "stick."

Here Wilber speaks about right view calling its attainment the "top-down approach." "Because the alternative to living the already realized state is that they become a seeker [bottom up]. And a seeker, of course, is somebody who relates to the world in terms of a fundamental lack, who presupposes a lack of Spirit, a lack of already enlightened self. All of that is in the contracted realm. But to the extent that they can stay aligned with that already liberated self—that's the top-down model—it starts reconfiguring their entire psychology.... So the top-down approach is important because a person has to really get a fundamental orientation [right-view] to the already liberated nature of their present condition. And that true awakening becomes the foundation of true spiritual practice and replaces the disposition of egoic seeking."[13] The Point of Power Practice is a top-down approach in the context of Simple Reality. It will work!

Right view inevitably shows up in our mythology. Edward Edinger says, "History and anthropology teach us that a human society cannot long survive unless its members are psychologically contained within a central living myth. Such a myth provides the individual with a reason for being. To the ultimate questions of human existence it provides answers which satisfy the most developed and discriminating members of the society. And if the creative, intellectual minority is in harmony with the prevailing myth, the other layers of society will follow its lead and may even be spared a direct encounter with the fateful question of the meaning of life."[14] However that myth or story must be a profound one to enable humanity to cope with self-created suffering.

Edinger continues: "It is evident to thoughtful people that Western society no longer has a viable, functioning myth. Indeed, all the major world cultures are approaching, to a greater or lesser extent, the state of mythlessness. The breakdown of a central myth is like the shattering of a vessel containing a precious essence; the fluid is spilled and drains away, soaked up by the surrounding undifferentiated matter. Meaning is lost. In its place, primitive and atavistic contents are reactivated. [Atavistic means the reappearance of characteristics in an organism after several generations of absence.] Differentiated values disappear and are replaced by the elemental motivations of power and pleasure, or else the individual is exposed to emptiness and despair. With the loss of awareness of a transpersonal reality (God), the inner and outer anarchies of competing personal desires take over."[15] In secular terms the "transpersonal reality (God)" is Simple

Reality and, of course, "competing personal desires" are the energy centers of the false self.

P-B is what Edinger calls "mythlessness" and he realized, as most of us do, that it is an unsustainable story. "The loss of a central myth brings about a truly apocalyptic condition and this is the state of modern man. Our poets have long recognized this fact. Yeats gave it a stark expression in his poem, 'The Second Coming.'"

> *Turning and turning in the widening gyre*
> *The falcon cannot hear the falconer [intuition];*
> *Things fall apart; the center cannot hold;*
> *Mere anarchy is loosed upon the world.*[16]

The world's religions are based in myth but religion has not interpreted mythology in a profound way and therefore right view is not understood in those contexts. Edinger agrees that: "The psychological approach to religious imagery is not available at any depth to one who is contained in a particular religious myth."[17] Religion does not encourage profound paradigm shifts and atheism is equally unsupportive of attaining right view. "If one is a religious believer he will be afraid to acknowledge his unconscious doubt. If one has no religious beliefs he will be afraid to admit his sense of spiritual emptiness."[18]

Religion and right view are not incompatible if one's religion is held in the context of Simple Reality. "When you are aware of the existence of the entity [Self] and of the soul, you can consciously draw upon their greater energy, understanding and strength." Seth continues: "It is *inherently* available, but your conscious intent brings about certain changes in you that automatically trigger such benefits. The results will be felt down to the smallest cells within your body, and will affect even the most seemingly mundane events of your daily life."[19] Religious mystics, aware of the right view, can assist all religions in discovering Simple Reality.

Jung "…also points out that the archetypal theme of the death of God is a part of the Christian myth. 'Christ himself is the typical dying and self-transforming God.' Christ died but he was not to be found in his tomb. 'Why seek ye the living among the dead? He is not here; he has risen.' Luke 24:5"[20]   We will not find our Christ Consciousness [right view or P-A] within the tomb (P-B).

The Buddha taught that we must have "…the correct view [and that it] is so important to go beyond conceptual understanding to the direct realization [insight] of the Absolute, awakened state."[21]   We will know when we have attained the Absolute, awakened state when our life has become a meditation and Simple Reality is the context for our life.

Chapter Twenty Four

The Collective Unconscious

An Awareness Of Sub-Conscious Influences On Our Behavior Is Essential To The Attainment Of True Freedom

The collective unconscious, identified by C. G. Jung, is a universal behavioral influence and is therefore an aspect of P-B, the self-destructive story in which humanity is contained. The historical significance of this idea in psychology is that Jung disagreed with Freud who held that the unconscious was exclusively personal and was composed of repressed childhood traumas. Jung discovered that the collective unconscious was a deeper layer beneath the personal unconscious.

The collective unconscious is not based on personal experience nor is it acquired. It is as if we are born into a pre-existing narrative common to all of humanity (P-B). The contents of this narrative consist of archetypes and patterns of instinctual behavior such as the seeking of security, sensation and power.

Ken Wilber helps flesh out our definition. "The content of the collective unconscious includes archetypes flowing from another source of that content, [namely] myths. These basic or primordial images represent very common, very typical experiences that humans everywhere are exposed to: the experience of birth, of the mother, the father, the shadow …the ego, the animus and anima, etc… Millions upon millions of past encounters with these *typical situations* have, so to speak, ingrained these basic images into the collective psyche of the human race. You find these basic and primordial images worldwide, and you find an especially rich fund of them in the world's great myths."[1]

The existence of the collective unconscious has been corroborated by the work of Joseph Campbell in his study of mythology. "Scholars have found Jung's understandings of symbols of the collective unconscious compatible with symbols in the writings of the great Spanish mystics, John of the Cross and Teresa of Avila."[2]

There is also a collective *identity* determined by the collective unconscious that Seth helps to clarify: "The mass race consciousness, in its terms, possesses an identity. You are a portion of that identity while still being unique, individual and independent. You are confined only to the extent that you have chosen physical reality, and so placed yourself within its context of experience."[3] One of Seth's mantras is that we "create our own reality" and by continually choosing reactions within P-B we create the "mass race consciousness" of suffering.

Seth continues: "There is a constant interplay between yourself and others in the exchange of ideas, both telepathically and on a conscious level.... You react only to those telepathic messages that *fit in with your conscious ideas* about yourself and your reality.... Let me add that the conscious mind is itself spontaneous. It enjoys playing with its own contents, so I am not here recommending a type of stern mental discipline in which you examine yourself at every moment."[4] Here I disagree with Seth in that we do need a discipline or practice and we do need to be continuously present to choose response over reaction using The Point of Power Practice from moment to moment.

The importance of having a healthy and receptive paradigm in supporting sustainable human behavior is stressed by Seth. P-A is friendly to healthy guidance from our interior wisdom. On the other hand in P-B, "It [the mind] will often neglect any clairvoyant or precognitive material that comes into the conscious mind from the deeper portions of the self. On occasion, when the ego recognizes that such data can be highly practical, it then becomes more liberal in its recognition of it—but only when such information fits in with its concepts of what is possible and not possible."[5] In P-B transcendence is not possible and we are left at the mercy of our reactive identity determined by both the personal unconscious and the collective unconscious.

"On closer examination one is always astonished to see how much of our so-called individual psychology is really collective. So much, indeed, that the individual traits are completely overshadowed by it."[6] Jung has identified a serious problem in P-B and that is that humanity behaves more like unconscious sleepwalkers than healthy, serene, and consciously aware individuals.

Most of humanity is choosing to conform to life within P-B and thereby losing contact with the inner wisdom from which we would derive our uniqueness and our ability to respond rather than react to life's experiences. "This sequence of events is inevitable once the individual combines with the mass and suppresses the development of selfhood or individual uniqueness."[7]

Jung continues to describe the influence of the collective unconscious and human behavior that resembles that of automatons or zombies more than self-realized human beings. "Society is organized, indeed, less by law than by the propensity to imitation, implying equally suggestibility, suggestion, and mental contagion…they are content to ape some eminent personality, some striking characteristic or mode of behavior, thereby achieving an outward distinction from the circle in which they move…. As a rule these specious attempts at individual differentiation stiffen into a pose, and the imitator remains at the same level as he always was, only several degrees more sterile than before."[8]

And in closing Jung reminds us of the importance of self-reliance and non-conformity that was advocated by the American transcendentalists Thoreau and Emerson. "A form of transformation experience is described which occurs when an individual identifies with a group of people who have a collective experience of transformation. This type of experience is distinguished from participation in a transformation rite, which does not necessarily depend upon, or give rise to, a group identity. Transformation as a group experience is described as taking place on a lower level of consciousness than transformation as an individual, because the total psyche emerging from a group is more like the animal psyche than the human. Although the group experience is easier to achieve, it does not cause a permanent change once the individual is removed from the group. Events in prewar Germany are cited as typifying the results of inevitable psychological regression which takes place in a group when ritual is not introduced to counteract unconscious instinctuality. Although this evaluation of mass psychology is conceded to be essentially negative, it is pointed out that the mass can also have positive effects by fostering courage and dignity; however, these gifts are considered to become dangerous if they are taken for granted and stifle personal efforts to achieve them."[9]

There is no need to seek or depend on any group, savior or guru. We are equipped with all that is necessary for self-reliant transformation or transcendence. Indeed, if we wait for a general or communal awakening or paradigm shift to begin we might be waiting for a long time indeed. The mass of humanity is mesmerized by a very powerful false self immersed in a collective unconscious that has a powerful negative influence on the human story. Don't wait within P-B for a change to begin, take the initiative and begin the Point of Power Practice today.

In Simple Reality, we embrace Oneness as our new worldview. With the help of our meditation practice we stop identifying with the mind, body and emotions, and attain a new identity. And finally, using the Point of Power Practice, choosing response over reaction, we transform our behavior and begin to transcend the influences of both the false self and the collective unconscious. This is truly the liberation we all seek!

Chapter Twenty Five

Buddha And Christ

Two Sides Of The Same Coin

Hindus use the term *avatar* to designate the incarnation of a deity in human form. In Simple Reality there are no anthropomorphic gods or supernatural beings separate from the rest of Creation. Therefore, it could be said that we are all *avatars* or embodiments of the creative impulse of the implicate order. In that sense, we all possess "Buddha-hood" or "Christ Consciousness."

There have been many phenomenal people who throughout history have accomplished remarkable things but there are two who stand out whose accomplishments have mesmerized their fellow human beings. By mesmerized I mean that these two individuals had an aura, so distinctive that people asked them, not "Who are you?" but "What are you?" These two people were Jesus Christ (from Christos, the anointed one) and Buddha. Buddha responded "I am awake" and his reply derived from the Sanskrit root *budh* meaning both to "wake up" and "to know," hence his title "Buddha" means the "Awakened One" or the "Enlightened One."

We could also describe these two individuals as charismatic, that is to say, they had an uncommon energy. As you might expect, I would explain this energy as P-A energy and that these two individuals were simply "present." They had shifted from P-B to P-A. They had stopped the constant reaction that characterizes most of our lives and found themselves in their "natural" state—the Now.

If we look at these two individuals from within the context of P-B they represent an interesting contrast between the Western view and the Eastern view of the fundamental human narrative. Both were teachers who sought to challenge P-B and both advocated a new story which they knew would drive a new identity for humanity and a resultant change in behavior. They each had a different approach to achieve their goal which was appropriate for their respective cultures and their contrasting personalities. These are the some of the principles and the practices that distinguish these two remarkable teachers and also what they had in common.

In Common	**Jesus (West)**	**Buddha (East)**
Teachers	Love	Law
Enlightened	Outer	Inner
Seekers	Personal	Impersonal
P-A Identity	Mysticism	Science
Epiphanies	Prayer	Meditation
	Jesus-baptism	Buddha-Insight at Bodh Gaya
	Messianic	Methodical
	Temptations	(False self energy centers)

It is very important to understand that humanity today, for the most part, does not understand the profound message of these two teachers. Each of these two men is seen as a founder of two of the world's great religions and yet both were opposed to that happening. They each knew that if their all-important teachings were lost in a cult of personality that they would be elevated to the status of divine religious beings. Concerning Buddha, there were attempts during his lifetime to turn him into a god. "He rebuffed all these categorically, insisting that he was human in every respect."[1] He was candid about his own human failings and about the difficulty of attaining enlightenment. This humanness no doubt made him more accessible and influential among his followers.

When their extraordinary human achievements (a paradigm shift) occurred and they were elevated beyond the ordinary human experience, the exact opposite of what each of these compassionate men had hoped to achieve occurred. They become not the wonderful example of what we as human beings can all achieve but the great exception which then seems beyond our ability to emulate. The very religions based on their teachings then are less effective in becoming supportive environments in which "heaven on earth" or "Nirvana" can be achieved. Their teachings become absorbed in and distorted by P-B and humanity becomes disempowered and confused rather than encouraged by what they demonstrated.

Buddha

Hiroyuki Itsuki in his book *Tariki: Embracing Despair, Discovering Power* "...describes the historical Buddha as initially the ultimate negative thinker. He abandoned the life of princely luxury at the age of twenty-nine in his spiritual quest and—after attaining enlightenment—taught the four noble truths, asserting that [at] the outset we have no control over our birth, old age, illness or death. He spread his teaching for forty-five years all over northern India and passed away under the twin sala trees with a smile on his face and said, 'The world is wonderful.' This Buddha, Itsuki posits, was [also] the ultimate positive thinker.... In practical terms the ultimate negative thinker lives without expectations....To have a supple, flexible mind means to affirm both hope and despair, success and failure, feeling the anxiety and the joy of living, all of which are necessary for us to become truly human....to celebrate the strength to live, feel the joy of life, and experience 'a sense of peace even though one still endures suffering and anxiety.'"[2]

Buddha shifted to P-A and thereby, being present, was able to choose response over reaction, intuitively understanding the Point of Power Practice. His life had become a meditation on the nature of reality. He demonstrated that enlightenment is experiencing the perfection of the Now.

"Letting the [present] moment take over is the practice of great honesty. To let the moment take over, you have to have great confidence in your true nature; the Buddha within you. When you find the Buddha within, everything is celebration. You will be able to see everything outside of yourself as the expression of the Buddha within. If something appears wrathful, it is understood as the expression of the Buddha within. If something appears peaceful, it is understood as the expression of the Buddha within. After all, everything is the expression of the Buddha within. Therefore, everything is your creation. Your creation is everything."[3] Shyalpa Rinpoche has just described our identity in P-A. He is also acknowledging that we create our own reality by projecting that identity onto the world of form. You can then see how important it is to have a wholesome identity, an identity in alignment with reality—in short an identity that is defined by a sustainable narrative—an identity that is first and foremost an expression of compassion.

We can see Buddha as the founder of psychology, the science of the human mind. He understood that the chief barrier to our natural state was the reactivity of the mind, the illusion that we are contained in the P-B narrative. Dzogchen Ponlop Rinpoche says that: "All the teachings of the Buddha exist for the purpose of developing the penetrating knowledge that sees through this illusion and wakes us up. It is important to realize that these teachings do not constitute a religion in the conventional sense. Rather they represent a genuine science of mind, a science of insight that uncovers the pure nature of the mind and world that we experience. They also portray a philosophy of life, a way to live life, which deals with its meaning and helps us understand how we can overcome the suffering of the world."[4]

We have all heard that the essence of Buddha's teaching is the Four Noble Truths. In the contemporary language of Peter Russell, they could be stated thusly:

I   We all experience suffering in one way or another—mental, physical, emotional or spiritual.
II We create our own suffering. It is a consequence of our cravings and aversion of our desiring things to be other than they are.

III It need not be this way. We have a choice as to how we perceive the world and live our lives.
IV There are systematic ways to go about changing how we think and perceive.[5]

I would describe the Four Noble Truths in this way:

1) As individuals or in collectives we are living in an unsustainable way in P-B. We are self-destructing on this planet.
2) The cause of this suffering or the source of this self-destructive energy is the context, narrative, paradigm or worldview (P-B) within which humanity derives its identity. We must change our beliefs, attitudes, values and reduce our emotional reactions.
3) The way out of this self-made illusion is to shift to a paradigm contained in the context of the present moment (the Now) which also will result in a new identity.
4) The way to measure if we have done this is to experience the distinction between feeling and emotions, intuition and intellect, and response and reaction. Compassion, peace, joy, and freedom and in religious terms—heaven—only exist in the Now. The ego, the "I," suffering, hell, original sin, the shadow, neurosis, and existential fear cannot enter the Now because they do not exist. Only the timeless, the true reality, Simple Reality exists.

The shift from P-B to P-A is difficult only in the sense that we must overcome the enormous inertia of our survival strategy conditioning, the collective unconscious, and other elements of our conscious and unconscious nature. We must come to "feel" the nature of reality and not get trapped by the need of our false self to have everything be "logical" in the P-B sense. The conventional logic of the intellect can be transcended and a much deeper more profound understanding of reality can be achieved.

One of the most radical truths which the Buddha taught and which challenged the old and illusionary logic is the absence of a separate self, an "I" or "me." "…'I,' is impermanent in nature and does not exist inherently; it is empty of any true, solid existence. Therefore, in his first teachings on emptiness, Buddha taught the nonexistence of a personal self or individual ego on the ultimate level.... Therefore, without realizing egolessness, there is no way one can achieve any degree of freedom... but *all* phenomena are empty as well. This means that the totality of our experience—both subjective and objective—is empty of true existence. All living experiences—from our thoughts, emotions, and perceptions to the appearances of external forms and events—have no solid basis in ultimate reality."[6] Dzogchen Ponlop Rinpoche has helped us understand that in the context of P-A, the wonderful freedom that comes with no longer identifying with the personal ego (including mind, body and emotions) is automatically felt and understood. Again, it is not difficult, just very different—very unfamiliar.

When we say that shifting to the present moment is not difficult, we know that many of you will not believe it because the P-B story tells us that all worthwhile attainments in P-B require great effort over time and often require a great deal of knowledge. The Buddha also fell into this trap and had to learn the hard way that P-A is our natural state. When we stop all of the having, doing and knowing—striving for security, sensation and power—we will find ourselves in the Now. "For some years before his enlightenment night, Buddha tried all sorts of extreme practices. He meditated on bliss, peace, and happiness. When this did not produce the lasting change he sought, he meditated on spaciousness, consciousness, nothingness, and on a state called neither-perception-nor-non-perception. When none of these profound trances helped, he tried ascetic practices. He stood on one foot in a lake with water up to his neck for days at time. He tried cow practice and dog practice—not speaking or bathing, and eating, sleeping, behaving, and vocalizing as if he were a cow or a dog. Next he tried hardly eating at all, till gradually he got down to one sesame seed a day. When none of these worked, he gave them up too."[7]

Buddha tried the practices described by Zoketsu Norman Fisher and many more over a period of six years. And, of course, when he gave them up he stopped reacting, relaxed, breathed and responded to the reality of the present moment. It is not any more difficult than that.

Christ

The Christ that we encounter in this chapter is not Christ the Savior commonly understood in the Christian religion. From a psychological standpoint Christ was one in a long line of universal archetypes. From a mystical point of view all of humanity has the potential for Christ consciousness which is compassionate human behavior in P-A.

To understand the significance of Christ we will rely on profound thinkers and mystics in touch with their intuitive or inner wisdom. We will not bother with the illusion of Christ the Savior found in P-B because that is precisely what we need to transcend. Starting with a paragon of compassion and a brilliant scholar who studied the life of the historical Jesus we find that "...the renowned genius and humanitarian Dr. Albert Schweitzer, in *The Quest for the Historical Jesus,* says that after years of careful study, he concluded there was no *traditional* [P-B] Jesus of Nazareth as a historical person."[8] If the "traditional" Jesus of the Bible was created by the early church fathers for essentially political reasons, who is the Christ that mythology, the mystics and psychology talk about?

Tom Harpur's research supports an important fact about Christianity. Christ existed before Jesus was born. "...no contemporary non-Christian writer even knew of Jesus' existence. It's for this reason that [mystics and some scholars were] able to declare Jesus a mythical person, the product of myth-making tendencies common to religious people of all ages, particularly the period of the early Roman Empire... 'Jesus is a radically Christianized version of the supernatural [hero] Joshua.... The Gospel editors thus did not have to invent Jesus, or Yeshua. His name was already in the air. He was already in the documents they had re-edited or transcribed. But later ignorance changed him from a symbol (type) to a personal entity or reality.... The Evangelists then, I am convinced, simply brought out to more popular knowledge hidden Gospels that already had a Joshua/Jesus central figure and had previously been concealed inside the depths of Essene and Mystery cult secrecy. They were an esoteric popularization, not a fresh literary or religious creation."[9]

Now let's connect, with Harpur's help, our mythical Jesus to the universal First Noble Truth of Buddha. "The evidence is overwhelming that in Paganism and early Christianity, the cross was always a symbol of life, never of death (except as "death," in its symbolic sense, means incarnation). To be in the body [P-B] was to be put—even impaled or crucified—on this cross of fleshly existence. This is the powerful meaning behind Jesus' command 'Take up your cross...'—that is, accept the discipline and ambiguity and suffering involved in being a fully aware human being. (The Greeks said that the body is the tomb of the soul, and they had a word play on it: *soma* [body] = *sema* [tomb].)"[10] Jesus was preaching surrender to reality as a first step to the paradigm shift. He knew the necessity of distinguishing between reaction and response before one could enter P-A.

Even Paul, the character so central to the unfolding of the Christian myth, has been profoundly misunderstood and his message also was twisted to fit P-B. "All his [Paul's] language about being 'in Christ' or having 'Christ in you" reflects the current Hellenic theosophy and philosophy. It is really Orphic-Platonic-Mystery cultism, almost pure Hindu or Vedic yoga mysticism, with no immediate reference to the Gospel life of Jesus at all. It is the universal Good News of the incarnation of the divine in every human being."[11] Paul's teaching, like that of Jesus, was the universal Good News of the reality of P-A—simple, not complex; easy, not difficult; and available immediately, not in some remote future time and space.

So how was the wonderful message that held the key to alleviate human suffering lost and remain so today? The P-B worldview cannot accommodate the principle of Oneness that is necessary to understand Christ's central message. Notice the not so subtle difference between the P-A interpretation of the meaning of his life and that of P-B. "The great truth that the Christ was to come *in man*, [P-A] that the Christ principle was potentially in every one of us, was changed to the exclusivist teaching that the Christ had come *as man* [P-B]."[12]

The mistake the early disciples made, and it was a grievous one, was to fail to understand Jesus' message concerning God's presence (the

Now). Thomas Sheehan put it succinctly. "They remade God's presence-among-men into God's presence-yet-to-come and eventually into Jesus himself... at this earliest stage of Christology, the disciples were in fact beginning the process of undoing Jesus' message by reconstituting an apocalyptic future... when he would supposedly bring what in fact he had already brought."[13] And from a very different perspective, Seth reminds us that "...the Christ personality said, '...the kingdom of God is *within* (among) you.' (Luke 17:21)."[14] In other words, "the kingdom of heaven is within" and "the kingdom of heaven is now" two of Jesus' key pronouncements became the "kingdom of heaven is out there and on its way." "You will have to work very hard, be very good, and wait very patiently." Ironically, those very P-B behaviors would effectively block any chance that we would attain our natural state of perfection, a state which Jesus had skillfully demonstrated.

Now we turn to Jung, who uses the language of Christianity, to better understand the universal significance of Christ. "Christ is of the opinion that whoever believes in him—believes, that is to say, that he is the son of God—can 'do the works that I do, and greater works [choosing response over reaction] than these.'"[15] Since we are all connected to the implicate order and the infinite energy of ongoing creation, Christ understood that we could continue the creative process as he had done. It was his fondest hope, however, that it would be within the context of the sustainable story of P-A.

Jung continues, "He reminds his disciples that he had told them they were gods. The believers or chosen ones are children of God and 'fellow heirs with Christ.' When Christ leaves the earthly stage, he will ask his father to send his flock a Counsellor (the 'Paraclete') [intuitive inner wisdom], who will abide with them and in them for ever. The Counsellor is the Holy Ghost, who will be sent from the father. This 'Spirit of truth' will teach the believers 'all things' and guide them 'into all truth.' According to this, Christ envisages a continuing realization of god in his children, and consequently in his (Christ's) brothers and sisters in the spirit, so that his own works need not necessarily be considered the greatest ones. Since the Holy Ghost is the Third Person of the Trinity and God is present entire in each of the three Persons at any time, the indwelling of the Holy Ghost means nothing less than an approximation of the believer to the status of God's son."[16]

That all of this would happen was predicated on humanity's understanding of the prerequisite paradigm shift. Failure to accept the new context, the new story advocated by Jesus (P-A) would mean that the "Good News" was null and void. And so far in the history of humanity, Christ's promise is yet to be fulfilled.

As some believe, Christ consciousness is within each person and can be brought to awareness with a process of Self-realization or in the case of Simple Reality, with a change in worldview or context. Jung would call the developmental Self-realization process "individuation." "In psychological terms, the incarnation of God means individuation. To the extent that one becomes aware of the transpersonal center of the psyche, the Self, and lives out of that awareness, one can be said to be incarnating the God-image. This experience involves encounter with the opposites. The Self is a union of opposites. When it first emerges into consciousness the opposites split apart and the ego is faced with the conflict of their opposition...."[17] This split between reality (P-A) and illusion (P-B) is represented concretely and described in this book in the chapters on Response and Reaction, Intuition and Intellect, and Feeling and Emotion.

"The hallmark of individuation is the differentiation of the individual psyche [self-reliance] from its containment in the collective psyche. This process is accompanied by a progressive awareness of the transpersonal psyche and the task of mediating and humanizing its energies. As soon as a more honest and more complete consciousness beyond the collective level has been established," writes Jung, "man is no more an end in himself, but becomes an instrument of God, and this is *really* so."[18] In terms of Simple Reality, becoming an instrument of God is experiencing the "flow" of the creative process in connection with the implicate order in the context of P-A. And this is *really* so!

Again, in Jung's Christian language, we have Christ teaching the vengeful and jealous Old Testament Jehovah how to be compassionate and capable of the unconditional love found in the New Testament God. "...Christ allows himself to be blasted by the wrath of God in order to redeem his fellow men. This sacrificial act not only redeems man but also transforms Yahweh. With his explosive rage spent by the innocent victim's voluntary acceptance of it, Yahweh is transformed into a God of love through the example of a loving man...."[19] This is also the significance and meaning of the story of Job in the Old Testament.

The Bible, both Old and New Testaments, is the story of the fundamental necessity of the shift from P-B to P-A before there can be any hope for a sustainable human community. In the words of Jung's worldview: "In other words, the ego is given the strength and purpose to stand against the primitive Self [false-self] through awareness of its sonship with the Self, which confers a sense of partnership in the mutual process of transformation."[20] And the next step, which even Jung failed to understand, is that once the ego has become healthier in realizing the self-destruction inherent in pursuing security, sensation and power, then it must realize its own insubstantial and ephemeral nature and surrender to the highest truth, the "no self" reality.

Christ, then, was our own true self projected onto an historical figure, Jesus of Nazareth, and given a personality that had compassion, wisdom and a profound sense of justice, the qualities that Yahweh, our "primitive" false self, lacked. He was, in short, more conscious. For those of us who understand that all of us *are* "Christ" the universe has become friendly and we are innocent. The transformation of God which is a reflection of the transformation of humanity can only occur in a more profound context because it is excluded in P-B. In other words, the paradigm must be profound enough to contain such a transformed consciousness.

Christ consciousness is nothing more than our own inner wisdom and is crucial in showing us how to live in the Now. "...since myths are part of the unconscious, they act as a bridge between the conscious and unconscious. Christ, as a combination of God and man archetypes, is part of this bridge."[21]   Jung continues, "The image of Christ as essentially androgynous, uniting the anima (soul) and the animus (consciousness), is stressed. In the human psyche the animus is still seen to symbolize consciousness, while the anima personifies the unconscious."[22]

In P-A, we have the powerful awareness or "presence" characteristic of what we could call Christ consciousness. Ken Wilber offers his inimitable and poetic description of that consciousness. "Ascent straight to the formless Godhead, *and* a perfect Descent to a loving embrace of the entire world of the Many—the standard message of all Non-dual schools: *transcend* absolutely every single thing in the Kosmos, *embrace* absolutely every single thing in the Kosmos—with choiceless compassion or love."[23]   This was the message of Christ and Buddha and remains their message today within each one of us where it has been from the beginning of our creation.

Chapter Twenty Six

Self-Reliance

*Within Each Of Us Is Everything Necessary
To Attain Our Highest Expression*

We forget the chain and we alone can break it.
        Vivekananda[1]

First I want to distinguish Self-reliance from self-reliance. The former is reliance on the True Self in a context of P-A. It is an acknowledgment of Oneness, the non-dual nature of Simple Reality. There is not a separate "self" in Self-reliance, no ego, no I. Reliance on the Universe (Essence, implicate order or True-self) is being in the present moment. In self-reliance the self in question is the ego, the false-self contained in the context of P-B. This self-reliance, of course, is based on illusion. To rely on the self is to experience the unending and certain betrayal by the conditioned mind of the false self.

Nevertheless, even this self-reliance has its relative benefits as we build a healthy ego and the confidence necessary to entertain a paradigm shift. A good analogy relating to the importance of gaining strength through self-reliance is that of the chick emerging from the egg. Any attempt to assist the chick and relieve it of what might seem a Herculean struggle to free itself from its hard-shelled prison would rob it of the very strength that it needs to survive once it emerges into a harsh world. The very process, of struggling to free itself is what develops the bodily strength to survive once it emerges from the egg.

In both the East and West there is a tradition of relying on others to negotiate what we can call religious or spiritual processes, whether it be salvation or Self-realization. Reliance on others leaves the spiritual aspirant powerless and even blocks the attainment of the ultimate goal. The minister, priest or guru can be helpful in the early stages of the spiritual path, however, at some point we must negotiate the final leg of the spiritual journey on our own in order to gain the strength necessary to attain the ultimate shift from P-B to P-A, to arrive at Self- Realization beyond duality and the illusion of form.

> *No other person can free a man from his bondage; he must do it himself."*[2]

"You are responsible for your own bondage. You are responsible for making your mind impure, no one else. You are responsible for purifying your mind, for breaking all the bondages. No one else can do that.[3] The good news about being totally responsible for creating what S. N. Goenka calls "bondages" is that if we created them, then we have the power to stop creating them. If we stop creating the bondages, they fall away and we gradually become free, free from all suffering, free from all cravings and aversions.

Attachment to the world of form and the ego's need to be continually having, knowing and doing is our "Achilles heel" so to speak. "…without devotion, faith or belief, without liking or inclination, without hearsay or tradition, without considering apparent reasons, without delight in the speculations of opinions, I know and see that the cessation of becoming is Nirvana."[4] As we learn in our initial meditation practice to stop identifying with body, mind and emotions, we gradually understand what is meant by "cessation of becoming." The following quote is from Buddha's *Sutta No. 7.*

"The closest translation of the word philosophy into Sanskrit is *darshana*, which literally means 'seeing' or 'experience,' referring to the mystical act of divine perception. Unlike Western philosophy, there is nothing speculative or abstract in Indian thought; it is based wholly upon direct and immediate perception of super-rational truth. Philosophers are, above all men of God who have discovered the wisdom of the Self through their own interior searchings. This is the true spirit of Indian religion."[5]

Nirvana; it has to be comprehended by the wise, each for himself.
Majhima-nikaya

Hindu mysticism speaks eloquently about Self-realization. "In one word, this ideal is that you are divine. 'Thou art That.' This is the essence of Vedanta. After all its ramifications and intellectual gymnastics, you know the human soul to be pure and omniscient; you see that such superstitions as birth and death are entire nonsense when spoken of in connection with the soul. The soul was never born and will never die, and all these ideas that we are going to die and are afraid to die are mere superstitions. And all such ideas as that we can do this, or cannot do that, are superstitions. We can do everything. Vedanta teaches men to have faith in themselves first. As certain religions of the world say that a man who does not believe in a Personal God outside himself is an atheist, so Vedanta says that a man who does not believe in himself is an atheist. Not believing in the glory of our own soul is what Vedanta calls atheism."[6]

Self-reliance is akin to skepticism as teachers of Zen realized. "First of all, they trusted doubt and rewarded questions. This is rare in religion and an example of the Zen way of treating what is usually thought of as a problem—in this case, doubt—as a strength....A question is a place of embarkation, and any question was treated as being about enlightenment, whether the student was aware of it or not. There was a trust in whatever forces had brought the student to the point of asking."[7]

Joseph Campbell synthesized religion and mythology to come up with his discoveries concerning human intuition. Self-reliance "...is based on the realization that Buddha-knowledge is achieved intuitively, by sudden insight... Look within! The secret is within you."[8]

C. G. Jung aids in our transition from East to West and helps to deepen our understanding of Self-reliance. "The Christian West considers man to be wholly dependent upon the grace of God, or at least upon the Church as the exclusive and divinely sanctioned earthly instrument of man's redemption. The East, however, insists that man is the sole cause of his higher development, for it believes in 'self-liberation.' ...[In the West] Grace comes from elsewhere; at all events from outside. Every other point of view is sheer heresy. Hence it is quite understandable why the human psyche is suffering from undervaluation."[9]

As Jung continues we can see that the Eastern worldview is much closer to P-A and the West is more closely identified with a P-B focus on the illusory world of form. "With us, man is incommensurably small and the grace of God is everything; but in the East, man is God and he redeems himself.... The East bases itself upon psychic reality, that is, upon the psyche as the main and unique condition of existence.... It is a typically introverted point of view, contrasted with the equally typical extraverted point of view of the West. ...Introversion is felt here as something abnormal, morbid, or otherwise objectionable. Freud identifies it with an autoerotic, 'narcissistic attitude of mind. In the East, however, our cherished extraversion is depreciated as illusory desirousness, as existence in the *samsara,* the very essence of the ...chain which culminates in the sum of the world's sufferings."[10]

Christianity was a key element in Jung's worldview and colors all aspects of his understanding of Self-reliance. "Although the Paraclete [Holy Ghost or True Self] is of the greatest significance metaphysically, it was, from the point of view of the organization of the Church, most undesirable, because as is authoritatively stated in scripture, the Holy Ghost is not subject to any control. In the interests of continuity and the Church the uniqueness of the incarnation and of Christ's work of redemption has to be strongly emphasized, and for the same reason the continuing indwelling of the Holy Ghost is discouraged and ignored as much as possible. No further individualistic digressions can be tolerated. Anyone who is inclined by the Holy Ghost towards dissident opinions necessarily becomes a heretic, whose persecution and elimination take a turn very much to Satan's liking. On the other hand one must realize that if everybody had tried to thrust the intuition of his own private Holy Ghost upon others for the improvement of the universal doctrine, Christianity would rapidly have perished in a Babylonian confusion of tongues—a fate that lay threateningly close for many centuries."[11] Traditional religion does not find mystics, iconoclasts or Self-reliant people acceptable.

As Rollo May points out, "One is good to the extent that one obeys the dictates of society and church [precepts]. An uncritical view of the Adam myth, of course, makes a very good rationalization for such tendencies—one can point out that if Adam had not disobeyed, he would never have been forced out of paradise. ...Thus a premium is implicitly placed on *not* developing consciousness of one's self. It is as though the more unquestioning obedience the better, and as though the less personal responsibility the better."[12]

> *Nothing has ever been more insufferable for man than freedom!*
> The Grand Inquistor in *The Brothers Karamazov* by Fyodor Dostoevsky

"One of the most remarkable pictures of the conflict between ethical sensitivity and existing institutions [P-A] and of the anxiety which ethical freedom brings, is in Dostoevsky's story of the Grand Inquisitor.... Christ's mistake, says the Inquisitor, was that 'in place of the rigid ancient law,' he placed on man the burden of having 'with free heart to decide for himself what is good and what is evil,' and 'this fearful burden of free choice' is too much for man.... 'Didst thou forget that man prefers peace and even death, to freedom of choice in the knowledge of good and evil?'"[13] The knowledge of good and evil most profoundly understood is the choice between Simple Reality or life as usual, between P-A or P-B.

Jung was intuitive enough to often transcend the religious aspects of his worldview with brilliant insights into the nature of Simple Reality. "The modern man—or, let us say again, the man of the immediate present—is rarely met with, for he must be conscious to a superlative degree.... The man who has attained consciousness of the present is solitary....Every step forward means tearing oneself loose from the maternal womb of unconsciousness [P-B] in which the mass of men dwell.... Thus, he has become 'unhistorical' in the deepest sense and has estranged himself from the mass of men who live entirely within the bounds of tradition. Indeed, he is completely modern only when he has come to the very edge of the world, leaving behind him all that has been discarded and outgrown, and acknowledging that he stands before the Nothing out of which All may grow."[14]

Thomas Jefferson exhibited the kind of Self-reliance that we would all do well to emulate. "When Jefferson was in the White House, he put together a Bible for himself by going through the Gospels and cutting out a lot of the miracles and the parts he couldn't understand. Jefferson put together what he believed were the essential teachings of Jesus. ... Jefferson called his book *The Life and Morals of Jesus of Nazareth."*[15] Like Jefferson, we all have the ability to separate the wheat from the chaff, as it were, when we rely on our innate ability to stay in response to our life's experience.

As is implied in the phrase "The devil made me do it" many of us resist taking responsibility for our own behavior. "'If the Evil one does not exist then man alone is responsible.'" Quoting Bishop Graber, Bible scholar Uta Ranke-Heinemann concludes that: "Humans don't want to bear the sole responsibility; they'd prefer to bear none at all."[16] All too often religion would like to keep the congregation in the ego-state of a child because control and manipulation are easier. Those that are Self-reliant provide their own salvation.

> *You shall serve your Creator as if there were only one man in the world, only you yourself.*[17]

Psychology supports our ability to be more Self-reliant. The editors of *Great Books of the Western World* saw fit to emphasize that we have the power for self-transformation. "Even though human emotions may have instinctive origins and be innately determined, man's emotional responses seem to be subject to voluntary control, so that men are able to form or change their emotional habits."[18] They are referring to our ability to distinguish between reaction and response and to choose response.

Eric Fromm brings to mind the relationship among Self-reliance, a profound worldview, and the resulting identity. "...if a person has not succeeded in integrating his energies in the direction of his higher self, he canalizes them in the direction of lower goals; if he has no picture of the world and his position in it which approximates the truth [P-A] he will create a picture which is illusory [P-B] and cling to it...."[19] Without the guidance inherent in the narrative of Simple Reality humanity is stuck in the false-self survival strategy unable to avail itself of its own inner wisdom, its own capacity for Self-reliance.

Seth, however, reminds us of the limitations of the conventional treatment modalities of psychology and does not seem to think that conventional therapy is useful in the process of Self-reliance. "...psychoanalysis is simply a game of hide-and-seek, in which you continue to relinquish responsibility for your actions and reality and assign the basic cause to some area of the psyche, hidden in a dark forest of the past. Then you give yourself the task of finding this secret. In so doing you never think of looking for it in the conscious mind, since you are convinced that all deep answers lie far beneath—and, moreover, that your consciousness is not only unable to help you but will often send up camouflages instead. So you play that game....you are not fully conscious unless you are aware of the contents of your conscious mind. I am also emphasizing the fact that the conscious mind is equipped to receive information from the inner self as well as the exterior universe."[20]

From America's preeminent philosopher, Emerson, in his essay entitled "Self-reliance," we hear from one who appreciated inner wisdom. "A man should learn to detect and watch that gleam of light which flashes across his mind from within, more than the luster of the firmament of bards and sages."[21] In the distinctions involved regarding "related pairs," Emerson comes down on the side of intuition over intellect.

Even "conventional" philosopher (that is to say, he was not a mystic) John Locke warned how identifying with mind, body and emotions was an obstacle to Self-reliance. "Locke's philosophy hinged upon arguing for the ability of the individual to detach from the world, and from himself, and observe each objectively."[22] Again, the world of form revealed by the senses, having no substantial reality, is not where we can expect to find Simple Reality.

To choose to remain in P-B and to refrain from relying on oneself for self-transformation is to fall short of the full experience of life. "This is what Nietzsche meant by the 'will to live'—not simply the instinct for self preservation, but the will to accept the fact that one is one's self, and to accept responsibility fulfilling one's own destiny, which in turn implies accepting the fact that one must make his basic choices himself."[23]

We close this chapter on Self-reliance with Western mystics beginning with Judge Thomas Troward. "...but the final discovery cannot be made *for* you, you must each make it *for yourself,* therefore, 'he that hath ears to hear let *him hear.*'" For example in the parable of the Prodigal Son, "...The younger brother is the man, who, not realizing his own spiritual nature, lives on the resources of the lower personality, till their failure to meet his needs drives him to look for something which cannot thus be exhausted, and eventually he finds it in the recognition of his own spiritual being as his inalienable birthright, because he was made in the image and likeness of God [in other words perfect], and could not by any possibility have been created otherwise. 'Son, thou art *ever* with me, and all that I have *is* [not will be] thine...'"[24]

The importance of self-reliance and acknowledging our own inner wisdom is affirmed by many sources including Edgar Cayce. In reading 276-2 he says to train the child "to depend upon the divine that lies within."[25]

In 1893, three years after the "official" closing of the American frontier, historian Frederick Jackson Turner wrote his famous "Frontier Thesis." He contended that the frontier experience beginning during colonial times and extending to the 1890 closing of the geographical frontier has fostered a unique American character including independence and self-reliance. Today we have the frontiers of translation, transformation and transcendence which also create and require Self-reliance for those who can keep moving along the edge of that ever-unfolding ineffable experience.

Chapter Twenty Seven

Conditioning And Behavior Modification

True Freedom Involves Changing Our Deepest Conditioned Behaviors

Most of humanity behaves in reaction to events, in their environment or in their minds, over which they have little or no control. It would not be an overstatement to say that enslavement to this almost automatic behavior is the all too common human condition. Fortunately, those who wish to live differently have a choice.

> *We are what we repeatedly do.*
> Aristotle

We began learning our self-destructive behaviors, our bad habits, at birth. We began then to construct our survival strategy seeking to meet our needs related to security, sensation and power. However, for most of us we were never satisfied with initial successes and we soon constructed a very elaborate, largely unconscious, and unsatisfactory array of behaviors. Because most of us don't have a sustainable worldview, a healthy identity and are behaving in ways that fail to produce happiness, we sing the false-self lament: "Is that all there is, is that all there is."

Why is humanity bent on self destruction (P-B) with so little effort given to choosing alternative behaviors (P-A)? We might explain our mass-suicidal behavior on what we can call the "tyranny of the bells." We are all familiar with the experiments related to operant conditioning which won Russian physiologist Ivar Petrovich Pavlov (1849-1936) the 1904 Nobel Prize. He "conditioned" dogs to salivate in reaction to the ringing of a bell associated with the appearance of food. When the dogs were "conditioned" they would salivate upon hearing the bell even when the original food stimulus was no longer there. Humanity today hears the ringing of three bells in the tower of the false self. Enslaved by our security, sensation and power conditioning we salivate when we are unconsciously triggered by the cacophony of those bells that are driving us mad. We will not be able to hear the beautiful dulcet tones produced by the bells of the true self until we enter the inner chapel of the present moment. Until then we will remain whining dogs longing for the food that is not there, yipping and barking at an illusion.

When human organisms are born and enter the global village there are Pavlov's aplenty to begin ringing thousands of bells to insure that the human child learns to salivate *a la* P-B. Parents and priests, teachers and tax collectors, pastors and peers, siblings and sycophants – and so the conditioning goes. Woe be it unto that child who tries to hearken to the peel of a different bell, the melodious inner ringing, the celestial harmony, the gentle, peaceful tinkling of the salivation-free present moment. There is virtually no support for the child who wants to march to the beat of the heart rather than the hubbub in the head.

Few indeed are those people who discovered that they have a choice to transcend the ringing of the bells of security, sensation and power and respond instead to the resplendent waves of energy flowing from a truer, illusory-free reality. The melody of P-A does not demand an automatic reaction but instead offers an array of self-reliant responses that have their origin in compassion, peace, joy, harmony and freedom. When those choices are made, time and again, day in and day out, an individual finds the sound of the old bells begins to fade and a glorious silence ensues – more beautiful than the cacophonous, blaring, ear-splitting, shrill racket coming from a human community driven mad by the endlessly clanging bell that exists only in the conditioned human mind.

The way out of our false-self conditioning is to re-condition our behaviors and in so doing shift our paradigm. We can do that by employing the Point of Power Practice. Why is the Point of Power Practice so effective in modifying human behavior? First, it has what is called by psychologists a short feedback loop. That means, the consequences of our choices, our reactions or responses, are often instantaneous. Both the reward (feeling) and the suffering (afflictive emotions) are quickly experienced. The short feedback loop empowers us in our goal to change our behaviors, our false-self conditioning. Understanding the distinction between response and reaction we can begin to shift from fear-driven afflictive emotions to compassionate responses. We then have the experience of "feeling" rather than "emotion" and we spend more and more time living in the present moment and less in the nightmarish, anxiety-laden past/future narrative. We escape P-B little by little and we are free. We have entered the serene, quiet stillness – we are at peace.

Appendix A

Simple Reality: The 6-Step Program

1. I choose and I create my own reality.

2. I have created an unsustainable worldview.

3. My behavior has been conditioned by my survival strategy and I have spent my life seeking, security, sensation and power.

4. I no longer identify with my body, emotions or mind.

5. At the point of power, I create a new story, a new identity and I choose response over reaction, feeling over emotion, intuition over intellect, freedom over slavery.

6. Living in the present moment, I am perfect awareness living in a perfect story free from illusion and afflictive emotions.

Appendix B

Dialogue Guides For Discussing Simple Reality

One way to begin the shift from an unsustainable worldview with pervasive self-destructive behaviors is to begin to define and internalize an alternative narrative. The following dialogue guides can be used to facilitate community conversations with that goal in mind.

Conversation One

- Due to the process of "Globalization" there is now only one major culture, one dominant worldview, operating in the world today.

- The culture of the "global village" is unsustainable.

- The operational dynamic of human consciousness works like this: *Worldview drives Identity drives Behavior*

- The world's religions tend to work backward from behavior (the "thou shalt nots" of precepts like the Ten Commandments and The Eightfold Path). In other words they attempt to change behavior which changes identity which creates a new context, i.e. "Heaven on earth." History has proven the futility of trying to create a healthy, sustainable human community through fear.

- To change the behavior of an individual or a collective, the worldview must be changed first. Remember that a good working definition of worldview is a person's or a collective's feelings, beliefs, attitudes and values.

Recommended Reading:
Armstrong, Karen. *A History of God.* New York: Knopf, 1994.
Chopra, Deepak. *How to Know God.* New York: Random House, Inc., 2000.

Conversation Two

- To build a sustainable global culture requires a profound understanding of why human beings behave as they do. Such an understanding is the beginning of the process of changing that behavior.

- The structure of human consciousness contains these elements: an unconscious, repressed shadow; a false self survival strategy driven by the mostly unconscious need for security, sensation and or power; a personal unconscious; and a collective unconscious.

- We can remember the behavioral characteristics of the false self (sometimes called the psychological model) by associating each with Americans cities that can be said to exemplify dominant behaviors of each.

> *Security (accumulation of material things):*
> New York City and Wall Street
> *Sensation (includes addictions):* Las Vegas
> *Power:* Washington D.C.

Recommended Reading:
Keating, Thomas. *Open Heart. Open Mind.* New York: The Continuum Publishing Company, 1986.
Keyes, Ken. *Handbook to Higher Consciousness.* Berkley, California: Living Love Center, 1975.

Conversation Three

- The content of the shadow is made up of all the behaviors that we repressed because they were disapproved of by our parents, peers, teachers, family, etc.
- We are unconscious of our shadow content and it can emerge spontaneously giving rise to the term "Freudian slip." Obviously, we have no control over what, when or if shadow content will present itself.

- The collective unconscious is the influence that our communities have on our emotions, beliefs, attitudes and values. This content has accumulated since the beginning of ancient human self-awareness. Mythology and psychology are the disciplines that shed light on this content and its influence on our worldview and behavior.

Recommended Reading:
Zweig, Connie and Abrams, Jeremiah. *Meeting the Shadow: The Hidden Power of the Dark Side of Human Nature.* Los Angeles: Jeremy P. Tarcher, Inc., 1991.
Ford, Debbie. *The Dark Side of the Light Chasers.* New York: Riverhead Books, 1998.
Johnson, Robert. *Owning Your Own Shadow.* New York: Harper, 1991.
Jung, C. G. *The Portable Jung.* New York: Penguin Books, 1971.
Jung, C. G. *Psychology and Religion.* New Haven, Connecticut: Yale University Press, 1938.

Conversation Four
- The distinction between each of the related pairs will help with the understanding of the distinction between paradigms A and B. Those pairs include: response and reaction, intuition and intellect, and feeling and emotion.
- The related pairs are part of a simple and secular language that avoids the ambiguities and emotional reactions that can accompany religious or philosophical language.

Appendix C

Glossary

If you wish to converse with me define your terms.
Voltaire

The process of shifting paradigms involves enriching the vocabulary to support the opportunities for a more profound self-expression and experience of reality. These definitions are tailored to assist in understanding the content of Simple Reality and are not meant to be valid in P-B. Nothing is valid in P-B.

allegory	a figurative treatment of one subject under the guise of another such as the parables of the New Testament or Aesop's fables wherein various animals personify human virtues and vices.
analogy	a resemblance or similarity in some particulars between things otherwise dissimilar; a ground of comparison or inference that if two things agree or can compare with each other in some respects, they will likely agree in others, such as in tracing the analogy between the "heart and a machine."
anima and animus	the internalized images of the opposite sex, the soul-image in each person.
archetypes	are innate, inherited structures in the unconscious which contain preformed characteristics, personal qualities and traits shared with all other human beings.
atheism	indifference to a personal creator.

attitudes	are the positions we take in life. It is through these stances that we give meaning and understanding to all of our experiences.
aura	a distinctive air or quality that characterizes a person.
autopoiesis	from the Greek *auto* "self" and *poiesis* "making" hence "self-making" referring to the autonomy of self-organizing systems.
avatar	an incarnation of God in a human form, for example, Jesus of Nazareth.
awareness	is being mindful or conscious psychologically, a non-judgmental observation. It is the ability of the mind to observe without criticism. With this ability, one sees things without condemnation or judgment, without craving or aversion (spiritual).
beauty	the experience of beauty is an altered state of consciousness, an extraordinary moment of poetry and grace.
cognition	the new concept of cognition, the process of knowing, involves perception, emotion, and action—the entire process of life.
complexes	eternally recurring human patterns of behavior. An exaggerated or obsessive concern or fear.
consciousness	is psychic substance connected to an ego.
conversion	the process of disowning oneself or divesting oneself of ego in order to be filled with divine grace.

cybernetics	the science of control and communication in the animal and the machine (from the Greek *kybernetes* "steersman").
determinism	the philosophic doctrine that every act, event, and decision is the inevitable consequence of antecedents that are independent of the human will.
dialogue	from the Greek *dia* meaning "between" and *logos* meaning "word." Hence, dialogue means the sharing feelings, beliefs, attitudes and values between or among peoples.
dissociation	a split in the conscious process in which a group of mental activities breaks away from the mainstream of consciousness and functions as a separate unit, as if belonging to another person, i.e., the abnormal separation of related ideas, thoughts or emotions.
dualism	the view that the world consists of two fundamental entities such as mind and matter or forces such as good and evil or that man has two basic natures, the physical and the spiritual.
ecology	the science of relations between the organism and the surrounding world (from the Greek *oikos* ("household"). The new science of ecology (1866) enriched the emerging systemic way of thinking by introducing two new concepts—community and network.
ecosystem	a community of organisms and their physical environment interacting as an ecological unit.
emotion	is the body's reaction to your mind.

enlightenment	the state of an *illumined* mind that has "seen the light" or is equanimous because it sees things in a "new light." It is a mind that is free of attachments and is able to accept life as it is and live in the present moment.
epiphany	a sudden intuitive comprehension of reality, a shift or breakthrough.
equanimity	composure, the quality of being calm and even-tempered, i.e., in response.
evil	the avoidance of the paradigm shift by choosing to remaining unconscious and entrapped in the unsustainable old narrative with the old identity.
faith	is the intuitive feeling that a higher spiritual power is at work in the universe and in our personal lives.
forgiveness	is the ego surrendering all judgment of self and others in order to allow the healing power of inner serenity to manifest. I
gestalt	the German word for organic form (as distinct from *Form*, which denotes inanimate form). An irreducible perceptual pattern, in which the whole is more than the sum of its parts. (Which has become the key formula of systems thinkers.)
grace	derives from the Latin *gratis*, meaning "free," "with no price to be paid" hence, a gift.
group-think	is the practice of conforming to group ethics or cultural standards.
happiness	is a state of well-being where individuals are typically not motivated to change their state.

hypnogogic	pertaining to the state preceding sleep. (also the synonym hypnopompic).
impressionism	a form of art, literature and music in which the artist, writer or composer has an experience or "impression" of a profound truth and expresses it in his/her art form.
individuation	(1) the process of a person becoming whole and unique—aims at embracing the light and dark simultaneously to create a constructive relationship between the ego and the self (C. G. Jung's term for creating consciousness).
	(2) the process whereby a series of psychic contents—complexes and archetypal images—make connection with an ego and thereby generate the psychic substance of consciousness.
integration	to form into a whole; to reclaim, accept, and include what was previously separate from our "self." Integration means accepting yourself and your feelings as you are. When something is not integrated, it causes sadness, resistance and conflict.
integrity	is achieved with the integration of feelings, beliefs, attitudes and values with awareness.
intelligent design	the hypothesis that the universe was created by some purposeful being or principle of order, the opposite of chaos.
intuition	the power or faculty of attaining direct knowledge or cognition without rational thought.

liberation	is a level of experience beyond pleasure and pain, beyond judgments of good and bad and even beyond time/space.
materialism	the theory that physical matter is the only reality and that thought, feeling, mind, and will can be explained in terms of physical laws.
metaphor	a figure of speech (from the Latin metaphora = transfer) in which a term or phrase is applied to something to which it is not literally applicable in order to suggest a resemblance of some kind as in "the strong arm of the law." A different thing being spoken of as if it were the other thing as in "All the world's a stage."
mind	from the Buddhist perspective mind is a faculty or organ like the eye but instead of sensing colors and forms it senses the world of ideas and thoughts and mental objects. Mind is not spirit as opposed to matter (true in most religions and philosophies).
mindfulness	is a meditative awareness that cultivates the capacity to see things just as they are from moment to moment, a synonym for Simple Reality.
modernism	is the collective worldview that dominated the nineteenth century and earlier twentieth century, characterized by an emphasis on scientific certainty, linear rationality, materialism, and universal truths. The era before post-modernism, i.e. today.
mystic	one who has a present moment experience of reality.
mystical	an experience of Simple Reality beyond the P-B illusion "provided" by the intellect or the senses.

myth	is a psychological pattern of timeless validity, true always and everywhere in its archetypal nature. Myth and fable use unreal things to speak of real things; myth teaches divine truth (P-A) and fable teaches common sense and virtue (P-B).
negation	is to deny what is false [while] not knowing what is truth. [It is] to see the false in the false and to see truth in the false, and it is the truth that denies the false. You see what is false, and the very seeing of what is false is the truth.
neurosis	dysfunctions characterized by anxiety, compulsions, phobias, depressions, and dissociations.
noetic	from the Greek *nous*, which means mind or ways of knowing.
non-locality	A field independent of limitations of time and space within which consciousness and creation are connected and share energy and interact. The creative process involving the implicate order.
now	is your only point of access into the timeless, birthless, deathless and formless realm of Being. Ultimately the Now is the power of your consciousness prior to thought, prior to forms arising out of it. *http://members.surfeu.fi/wpk/links/Tolle/focus.*
pantheism	the world is a part of God.
panentheism	the world is a part of God, but God is more than the world.

parable	tells a story about common everyday things and at the same time draws a subtle analogy between the ordinary facts of the story and the deeper meaning which lies parallel to the facts; it is a simple story in which a moral lesson may be drawn; and it is usually an allegory.
paradigm	a constellation of concepts, values, attitudes, beliefs, emotions, perceptions, and practices shared by a community, which forms a particular vision of reality that is the basis of the way the community organizes itself, and from which individuals derive their identity.
paradigm shift	changes of paradigms occur in discontinuous, revolutionary breaks called paradigm shifts using the Point of Power Practice.
peak experience	(1) an almost overwhelming sense of pleasure, euphoria, or joy; a deep sense of peacefulness or tranquility; feeling in tune, in harmony, or at one with the universe; a sense of wonder or awe; altered perceptions of time and/or space. . . a deep feeling of love, a greater awareness of beauty;. . . a sense that it would be difficult to describe adequately in words. (2) living in the present moment or the Now.
Pentecost Sunday	the day Catholics believe the Holy Spirit came to give power to Christians soon after Jesus ascended to heaven.
persona	is a compromise between what society expects of us and our own personal identity, between individuality and self-image.

physics	from the Greek *physis* meaning "Nature." The science of matter and energy and the interactions between the two.
postmodernism	is characterized by a recognition of the severe limitations of science and by its own complex rationality, its humanitarianism, and its emphasis on the universal *relativity* of truth in all domains.
processing	is a psychological term that refers to the concept of accepting and staying with experience as it manifests, allowing it to unfold by itself in the here and now.
procrustean	after Procrustes, a mythical giant who stretched or shortened captives to make then fit his beds, hence producing conformity by ruthless or arbitrary means. Having merciless disregard for individual differences or special circumstances.
projection	seeing others as the source of my pain or happiness.
propaganda	the systematic propagation of a given doctrine or of allegations reflecting its views and interests.
psyche	is Greek for "soul."
psychology	the science of the "soul."
psychoneurosis	is the suffering of a soul which has not discovered its purpose or true identity.
reality	that which never changes or ceases to exist.
reframing	is a technique that means finding the proper context for any event, so that it is perceived positively rather than negatively.

religion	an organized system of beliefs and rituals centering on a supernatural being or beings.
repression	to keep out of the conscious mind.
sanity	comes from the Latin *sanus* meaning "whole" or "healthy."
schadenfreude	pleasure or the embarrassing (ashamed) reaction of relief we feel when something bad happens to someone else instead of us. From the German, schaden (harm) + freude (joy).
self	the psychological center of the human being, synonym for ego.
self-esteem	is the disposition to experience oneself as competent to cope with the basic challenges of life and as worthy of happiness.
self-realization	the complete development or fulfillment of one's own potential (psychological).
self-realization	the attainment of transcendent liberation (spiritual).
shadow	those elements of the self such as feelings, emotions, ideas, and beliefs with which we cannot identify, which are then repressed due to education, culture, or value system.
shadow work	the conscious and intentional process of integrating that which we have chosen to ignore or repress.

suffering	results from our resistance to pain. *The way I see it, if you want the rainbow, you gotta put up with the rain.*—Dolly Parton
sustainable society	a society that satisfies its needs without diminishing the prospects of future generations.
symbiosis	close coordination of activities among different species resulting in living systems having the characteristics of single organisms.
symbol	a symbol (from the Greek *symbolon*: "thrown together") expressing something irrational and indescribable in ordinary speech and language.
synchronicity	always deals with a thought, vision, dream or premonition that is non-causally connected to some outer event.
syndrome	a group of symptoms that collectively indicate or characterize a disease, psychological disorder, or other abnormal condition.
system	in both living organisms and social systems, an integrated whole whose essential properties arise from the relationships between its parts.
systems analysis	to look at the entire problem, as a whole, in context, and to compare alternative choices in the light of their possible outcomes.
systems thinking	the understanding of a phenomenon within the context of a larger whole. From the Greek *synhistanai* (to place together).
systemic	the holistic perspective and the way of thinking it implies called "systems thinking," sometimes used as a synonym of "ecological."

theism	God is separated from creation.
threshold	an illness, depression, or a failed relationship when the psyche is speaking through the body, mind, or the heart about the need for change, the opportunity to move forward on the spiritual path.
typology	the functions of consciousness.
Vedanta	is the philosophy of transcendental knowledge based on the teachings of the Vedas, the ancient, revealed scriptures of the Hindus.
virtue	*virtus*, in Latin, means "spiritual strength" Virtue, it is said, is its own reward. Virtues are therefore a form of preventative medicine.
war	the wars we engage in are compulsive rituals, shadow dramas in which we continually try to kill those parts of ourselves we deny and despise.
worldview	the feelings, beliefs, attitudes and values held by an individual or community of individuals.
zeitgeist	the taste or outlook characteristic of a period or generation.

BIBLIOGRAPHY

Books, Periodicals and Websites

Adam, Michael. *Wandering in Eden: Three Ways to the East Within Us.* New York: Knopf, 1976.
Aurelius, Marcus. *The Meditations of Marcus Aurelius.* New York: Avon, 1993.
Blau, Evelyn. *Krishnamurti: 100 Years.* New York: Stewart, Tabori and Chang, 1995.
Borysenko, Joan. *Guilt is the Teacher, Love is the Lesson.* New York: Warner, 1990.
Braden, Charles S. *Spirits in Rebellion: The Rise and Development of New Thought.* Dallas: Southern Methodist University Press, 1987.
Brome, Vincent. *Jung: Man and Myth.* New York: Atheneum, 1981.
Buber, Martin. *Martin Buber's Ten Rungs.* New York: Citadel, 1974.
Campbell, Joseph. *Creative Mythology.* New York: Viking, 1968.
Campbell, Joseph. *Hero With a Thousand Faces.* New York: Bollingen Foundation, Inc., 1949.
Campbell, Joseph. *The Hero's Journey.* New York: Harper, 1990.
Campbell, Joseph. *Myths To Live By.* New York: Bantam, 1973.
Campbell, Joseph. *The Power of Myth.* New York: Bantam, 1988.
Capra, Fritjof. *The Tao of Physics.* New York: Bantam, 1975.
Chopra, Deepak. *The Seven Spiritual Laws of Success.* San Rafael: Amber-Allen Publishing, 1994.
Davis, Thomas D. *Philolosophy.* New York: McGraw-Hill, 1993.
Durant, Will and Ariel Durant. *The Age of Voltaire.* New York: Simon and Schuster, 1965.
Edinger, Edward. *The Creation of Consciousness: Jung's Myth for Modern Man.* Toronto, Canada: Inner City Books, 1984.

Emerson, Ralph Waldo. *The Portable Emerson.* New York: Viking, 1946.

Errico, Rocco A. *Let There Be Light.* Marina del Rey, California: Devorss & Company, 1985.

Ferrucci, Piero. *Inevitable Grace.* Los Angeles: Tarcher, 1990.

Fields, Rick. *Chop Wood, Carry Water.* Los Angeles: Tarcher, 1984.

Foundation For Inner Peace. *A Course in Miracles Volume Three: Manual For Teachers.* Farmingdale, New York: Coleman Graphics, 1975.

Fox, Emmet. *The Sermon on the Mount.* New York: Harper, 1934.

Fox Matthew. *The Coming of the Cosmic Christ.* New York: Harper, 1988.

Fox, Matthew. *Original Blessings.* Sante Fe: Bear and Company, 1983.

Gaylin, Willard. *Adam and Eve and Pinocchio: On Being and Becoming Human.* New York: Penguin, 1990.

Gibran, Kahlil. *The Prophet.* New York: Knopf, 1923.

Guiley, Rosemary. *Harper's Encyclopedia of Mystical and Paranormal Experience.* San Francisco: Harper. 1991

Gunaratana, Henepola. *Mindfulness in Plain English.* Boston: Wisdom Publications. 1991.

Gyatso, Tenzin. *The Dalai Lama: A Policy of Kindness.* New York: Snow Lion Publications, 1990.

Harpur, Tom. *The Pagan Christ.* New York: Walker and Company, 2004.

Harrison, Steven. *Doing Nothing.* New York: Tarcher/Putnam, 1997.

Hart, William. *Vipassana Meditation as Taught by S. N. Goenka.* San Francisco: Harper, 1987.

Hartmann, Thom. *The Last Hours of Ancient Sunlight.* Northfield, Vermont: Mythic, 1998.

Harvey, Andrew. *The Essential Mystics.* San Francisco: Harper, 1998.

Hawkins, David. *The Eye of the I.* Sedona, Arizona: Veritas Publishing, 2001.

Hibbard, Addison, and Horst Frenz. *Writers of the Western World.* New York: Houghton, 1954.

Holmes, Fenwick L. *Ernest Holmes: His Life and Times.* New York: Dodd, Mead, & Company, 1970.

Holmes, Ernest. *How to Use the Science of Mind.* New York: G. P. Putnam's Sons, 1919.

Holmes, Ernest. *The Science of Mind.* New York: Dodd, Mead & Company, 1938.

Holmes, Ernest. *This Thing Called You.* New York: G. P. Putnam's Sons, 1948.

Hutchins, Robert Maynard [ed.], *Great Books of the Western World: The Great Ideas: A Syntopicon Vol. I.* Encyclopedia Britannica, Inc. 1952.

Johnson, Clive, *Vedanta. An Anthology of Hindu Scripture, Commentary, and Poetry.* New York: Bantam, 1971.

Johnson, Robert. *He: Understanding Masculine Psychology.* New York: Harper, 1989.

Johnson, Robert. *Transformation.* San Francisco: Harper, 1991.

Jung, C. G. *Abstracts of the Collected Works of C. G. Jung.* Rockville, Maryland: NIMH, 1978.

Jung, C. G. *Man and His Symbols.* New York: Doubleday, 1964.

Jung, C. G. *The Portable Jung.* New York: Penguin Books, 1971.

Kabat-Zinn, Jon. *Wherever You Go, There You Are.* New York: Hyperion, 1994.

Kato, Kay Mieno. *Buddhism for Everyday Living.* Denver: McGraw Printery, 1968.

Kavanaugh, Philip. *Magnificent Addiction.* Lower Lake, California: Aslan Publishing, 1992.

Larzelere, Bob. *The Harmony of Love.* San Francisco: Context Publications, 1982.

Magill, Frank N. ed. *Masterpieces of World Literature.* New York: Harper, 1989.

May, Rollo. *The Discovery of Being.* New York: W.W. Norton and Company. 1983.

May. Rollo. *Man's Search For Himself.* New York: Norton 1953.

Miller, Arthur. *All My Sons, et. al.* New York: Penguin Books, 1995.

Moore, Thomas. *Dark Nights of the Soul.* New York: Gotham, 2004.

Moyers, Bill. *Bill Moyers A World of Ideas.* New York: Doubleday, 1989.

Murck, Christian, ed. *Artists and Traditions: Uses of the Past in Chinese Culture.* Princeton, New Jersey, Princeton University Press, 1976.

Pearce, Joseph Chilton. "Evolution's End." *Science of Mind.* Los Angeles: June, 1993.
Peterson, Roland. *Everyone is Right.* Marina del Ray, California: DeVorss and Company, 1986.
Powell, Robert. *Why Does God Allow Suffering?* Berkeley, California: AHP Paperbacks, 1989.
Rahula, Walpola. *What the Buddha Taught.* New York: Grove Weidenfeld, 1959.
Ranke-Heinemann. Uta. *Putting Away Childish Things.* New York: Harper/Collins, 1994.
Rinpoche, Chogyam Trungpa. *Illusion's Game.* Boston: Shambhala, 1994.
Roberts, Jane. *The Nature of Personal Reality.* New York: Bantam, 1974.
Roberts, Jane. *Seth Speaks.* New York: Bantam, 1972.
Russell, Peter. *Waking Up in Time.* Novato, California: Origin Press, 1992.
Seldes, George. *The Great Thoughts.* New York: Random House, 1985.
Sheehan, Thomas. *The First Coming.* New York: Random House, 1986.
Sinetar, Marsha. *Ordinary People as Monks and Mystics.* New York: Paulist Press, 1986.
Smith, Huston. *The Religions of Man.* New York: Harper, 1958.
Stevens, Wallace. *The Necessary Angel.* New York: Knopf, 1942.
Sugrue, Thomas. *There Is a River.* New York: Holt, 1942.
Tauber, Alfred. *Henry David Thoreau and the Moral Agency of Knowing.* Los Angeles: University of California Press, 2001.
Teasdale, Wayne. *The Mystic Heart.* Novato, California: New World Library, 1999.
Tolle, Eckhart. *A New Earth.* New York: Dutton, 2005.
Tolle, Eckhart. *The Power of Now.* Novato, CA: New World Library, 1999.
Troward, Thomas. *Bible Mystery and Bible Meaning.* New York: Dodd, 1913.
Troward, Thomas. *Collected Essays of Thomas Troward.* Marina Del Rey, CA: De Vorss and Company, 1921.

Troward, Thomas. *The Edinburgh Lectures on Mental Science.* New York: Dodd, 1909.
Van der Post, Laurens. *Jung and the Story of our Time.* New York: Random House, 1975.
Wilber, Ken. *A Brief History of Everything.* Boston: Shambhala, 1996.
Wilber, Ken. *Sex, Ecology and Spirituality.* Boston: Shambhala Publications Inc., 1995.
Wilber, Ken, et. al. *Transformations of Consciousness.* Boston: Shambhala Publications, Inc., 1986.
Williamson, Marianne. *A Return to Love.* New York: Harper Collins, 1992.

Periodicals

Ardagh, Arjuna. "Cultivating Translucence." *Shift at the Frontiers of Consciousness.* Petaluma, September-November, 2005.
Armstrong, Karen. "Compassions Fruit." *AARP The Magazine.* March/April, 2005.
Barasch, Marc Ian. "You Are Not My Enemy." *Shift to the Frontiers of Consciousness.* Petaluma, California, June-August, 2005.
Bays, Jan Chozen. "Ultimately You're Healthy Relatively You Die." *Shambhala Sun.* Boulder, Colorado, May 2005.
Belitsos, Byron. "Neurotechnology's Shadow." *Shift: At the Frontiers of Consciousness.* Petaluma, California, September-November, 2007.
Bennett, *Venture Inward,* Virginia Beach: Association for Research and Enlightenment, January/ February, 2007, p. 48.
Boyce, Barry. "Mind, Matter, or God" *Shambhala Sun, Boulder, Colorado*, January, 2008.
Boyce, Barry. "Overcoming Shyness; Mindful Divorce." *Shambhala Sun.* January, 2002.
Boyce, Barry. "Two Sciences of Mind." *Shambhala Sun,* Boulder, Colorado, September, 2005.
Chopra, Deepak. ""The Healing Reality." *Science of Mind.* Los Angeles, November, 1989.
Cohen, Andrew and Ken Wilber. "the Guru and the Pandit, Breaking the Rules." *What is Enlightenment?* Lennox, Massachusetts, Fall/Winter, 2002.

Cohen, Andrew and Ken Wilber. "the Guru and the Pandit, Following the Grain of the Kosmos dialog V." *What is Enlightenment?* Lennox, Massachusetts, May-July, 2004.

Cox News Service. "Mood survey colors Britons blue." *The Denver Post.* October, 21, 2000.

DeQuincy, Christian. "Multimedia." *Shift: At the Frontier of Consciousness.* Petaluma, California, March-May 2005.

Dowd, Maureen. "America recovers from affluenza." *The Denver Post,* April 2, 2009.

Editor. "The New Paradigm of Connectedness." *Shift: At the Frontiers of Consciousness.* Petaluma, California, March-May, 2006.

Feinstein, David. "Subtle Energy: Psychology's Missing Link." *IONS Noetic Review,* Petaluma, California, June-August, 2003.

Ferguson, Gaylon. "Evaluating Eckhart." *Shambhala Sun.* Boulder, Colorado, July, 2008.

Fischer, Zoketsu Norman. "Coming Home to the Body." *Shambhala Sun.* Boulder, Colorado, July, 2008.

Fischer, Zoketsu Norman. "The Universal Technique." *Shambhala Sun.* Boulder, Colorado, September, 2001.

Freemantle, Francesca. "Another Reality." *Shambhala Sun.* Boulder, Colorado, November, 2004.

Galloway, Paul. "Genes drive our behavior, author argues." *The Denver Post.* No date.

Goenka, S.N. "The Buddha's Path Is For Experiencing Reality." *Vipassana Newsletter.* Vol. 29, No. 1, May, 2002.

Hahn, Thich Nhat. "For 30 Years the Best Buddhism in America: Meditation." *Shambhala Sun.* January 2010.

Harman, Willis in Institute of Noetic Sciences. *The 2007 Shift Report.* 2007

Harsanyi, David. "Don't stress on stress." *The Denver Post.* November 6, 2009.

Institute of Noetic Sciences. "The 2008 Shift Report." *Shift: At the Frontier of Consciousness."* Petaluma, March-May 2008.

Johnson, Charles. "The King We Need." *Shambhala Sun.* Boulder, Colorado, January, 2005.

Keepin, Will. "Science and Spirit: Integrating the Sacred and the Secular." *Timeline.* Palo Alto, September/October, 1998.

Lama, Dalai, His Holiness, The. "Contemplative Mind: Hard Science." *Shift: At the Frontiers of Consciousness.* Petaluma, California, December 2005—February, 2006.

Lawrence, Mac. "The Search for a Nonviolent Future." *Timeline.* November/December, 2002.

Malik, Karen, "Essence." *Shambhala Sun.* Boulder, Colorado, May 2006.

Matousek, Mark. "Stroke of Luck." *AARP Journal,* November/December, 2008.

May, Rollo. "Creativity." *Shift: At the Frontiers of Consciousness.* Petaluma, California, March-May 2005.

Nisker, Wes. "The Dharma and The Drama." *Inquiring Mind.* Barre, MA. (No date)

O'Connor, Colleen. "Needed: a revolution of the heart." *The Denver Post.* March 20, 2005.

Packer, Toni. "Toni Packer." *Shambhala Sun.* Boulder, Colorado, July, 2005.

Parry, Glenn Aparicio. "Native Wisdom in a Quantum World." *Shift: At the Frontier of Consciousness.* Petaluma, California, December 2005—February 2006.

Peterson, Anita Harkin. "Cayce Principles of Child Guidance." *Venture Inward.* Virginia Beach, January/February 1991, p. 38.

Phipps, Carter. "No escape for the ego." *What is Enlightenment?* Lennox, Massachusetts, Spring/Summer, 2000.

Phipps, Carter. "The cosmos, the psyche and You." *What is Enlightenment?* Lennox, Massachusetts, February/April, 2008.

Porterfield, Christopher. "Duel at the Tipping Point." *Time.* March 14, 2005.

Powell, Diane. "We Are All Savants." *Shift: At the Frontiers of Consciousness.* Petaluma California, December 2005-February 2006.

Rinpoche, Chogyam Trungpa. "Reflections in the Cosmic Mirror." *Shambhala Sun.* Boulder, Colorado, January 2009.

Rinpoche, Dilgo Khentse. "The Mind's True Nature." *Shambhala Sun.* Boulder, Colorado, January, 2009.

Rinpoche, Dzogchen Ponlop. "The Wisdom of the Body and the Search for the Self." *Shambhala Sun*. Boulder, Colorado, September, 2004.

Rinpoche, Dzogchen Ponlop. "What the Buddha Taught." *Shambhala Sun*. Boulder, Colorado, May, 2006.

Rinpoche, Dzongsar Khyentse. "Buddhism in a Nutshell." *Shambhala Sun*. Boulder, Colorado, March, 2000.

Rinpoche, Sakyong Mipham. "A Reign of Goodness." *Shambhala Sun,* Boulder, Colorado, September, 2005.

Rinpoche, Sakyong Mipham. "No Complaints." *Shambhala Sun*. Boulder, Colorado, November, 2004.

Rinpoche, Sakyong Mipham. "Seeing the Essence of Phenomena as Wisdom." *Shambhala Sun*. Boulder, Colorado, May, 2004.

Rinpoche, Shyalpa. "A Path of Honesty." *Shambhala Sun*. Boulder, Colorado, May, 2003.

Rinpoche, Tulka Urgyen. "Existence & Nonexistence." *Shambhala Sun*. Boulder, Colorado, March, 2000.

Ross, David. "The Light Enters You." *Shambhala Sun,* Boulder, Colorado, November, 2004.

Sahtouris. Elisabet. "Seven Reasons Why I Remain an Optimist." *Shift: At the Frontiers of Consciousness.* Petaluma, California, June-August, 2006.

Smith, A. Robert, "Science discovers the Akashic field." *Venture Inward.* July/August, 2008.

Squires, James. "Campaign '92.' *The Denver Post.* June 23, 1992.

Streett, Bill. "Science and the Reenchantment of the Cosmos: The Rise of the Integral Vision of Reality." *Shift: At the Frontiers of Consciousness.* Petaluma, California, June-August 2006.

Sullivan, Jim. "The Damage Done." *The Denver Post,* August 4, 1996.

Tarrant, John. "Paradox, Breakthrough, and the Zen Koan." *Shift: At the Frontiers of Consciousness.* Petaluma, California, March-May 2005.

Todeschi, Kevin J. "Oneness: The First Lesson." *Venture Inward,* May/June 1995.

Unno, Taitetsu. "The Power of Negative Thinking." *Shambhala Sun,* Boulder, Colorado, July, 2001.

Van Auken, John. [ed.] "In Our Womb of Consciousness." *Personal Spirituality.* June/July 2009.

Wilber, Ken. "Letters." *What is Enlightenment?* Lennox, Massachusetts, Spring/Summer, 1999.

Will, George. "America's conservative core runs broad and deep." *The Denver Post.* October 10, 2004.

Yogis, Jaimal. "Ride of a Lifetime." *Shambhala Sun.* Boulder, Colorado, March, 2006.

Websites

Bertrand, Michael.
   http://www.inner-growth.info/power_of_now_tolle/eckhart_tolle_interview_bertrand.htm
   "The Power of Now." September 30, 2002. An interview with Eckhart Tolle by Michael Bertrand.

Tolle, Eckhart. http://www.eckharttolle.com/home/

NOTES

CHAPTER 2 – Worldview
1. Larzelere, Bob. *The Harmony of Love.* San Francisco: Context Publications, 1982, 67.
2. Roberts, Jane. *The Nature of Personal Reality.* New York: Bantam, 1974, 356.
3. Institute of Noetic Sciences. "The 2008 Shift Report." *Shift: At the Frontier of Consciousness."* Petaluma, March-May 2008, 35.
4. Jung, C. G. *The Portable Jung.* New York: Penguin Books, 1971, 105.
5. Jung, C. G. *Abstracts of the Collected Works of C. G. Jung.* Rockville, Maryland: NIMH, 1978, 63.
6. Phipps, Carter. "The cosmos, the psyche and You." *What is Enlightenment?* Lennox, Massachusetts, February/April, 2008, 56.
7. Ibid, 62.
8. May. Rollo. *Man's Search For Himself.* New York: Norton 1953, 45.
9. Ibid, 152.
10. Magill, Frank N. ed. *Masterpieces of World Literature.* New York: Harper, 1989, 250.

CHAPTER 3 – Afflictive Emotions, Attitudes, Beliefs and Values
1. Rinpoche, Dzongsar Khyentse. "Buddhism in a Nutshell." *Shambhala Sun.* Boulder, Colorado, March, 2000, 41.
2. Roberts, Jane. *The Nature of Personal Reality.* New York: Bantam, 1974, 421-424.
3. Cox News Service. "Mood survey colors Britons blue." *The Denver Post.* October, 21, 2000.
4. Roberts, Jane. *The Nature of Personal Reality.* New York: Bantam, 1974, 307.

CHAPTER 4 – Identity
1. Rinpoche, Sakyong Mipham. "No Complaints." *Shambhala Sun.* Boulder, Colorado, November, 2004, 12.
2. Edinger, Edward. *The Creation of Consciousness: Jung's Myth for Modern Man.* Toronto, Canada: Inner City Books, 1984, 62.
3. Powell, Robert. *Why Does God Allow Suffering?* Berkeley, California: AHP Paperbacks, 1989, 15.
4. Edinger, Edward. *The Creation of Consciousness: Jung's Myth for Modern Man.* Toronto, Canada: Inner City Books, 1984, 38.

5   Ibid, 39.
6   Foundation For Inner Peace. *A Course in Miracles Volume Three: Manual For Teachers.* Farmingdale, New York: Coleman Graphics, 1975, 86.

CHAPTER 5 – True Self and False Self
1   Malik, Karen, "Essence." *Shambhala Sun.* Boulder, Colorado, May 2006, 32-33.
2   Ibid, 32-33.
3   Jung, C.G. *Man and His Symbols.* New York: Doubleday, 1964, 49.
4   Holmes, Ernest. *How to Use the Science of Mind.* New York: G. P. Putnam's Sons, 1919, 100.
5   Jung, C.G. *Man and His Symbols.* New York: Doubleday, 1964, 102.
6   Ferrucci, Piero. *Inevitable Grace.* Los Angeles: Tarcher, 1990, 241.
7   Tauber, Alfred. *Henry David Thoreau and the Moral Agency of Knowing.* Los Angeles: University of California Press, 2001, 7.
8   Dowd, Maureen. "America recovers from affluenza." *The Denver Post,* April 2, 2009, 15B.
9   Gibran, Kahlil. *The Prophet.* New York: Knopf, 1923, 33-35.
10 Kavanaugh, Philip. *Magnificent Addiction.* Lower Lake, California: Aslan Publishing, 1992, 68.
11 Sullivan, Jim. "The Damage Done." *The Denver Post,* August 4, 1996, 4E.
12 Galloway, Paul. "Genes drive our behavior, author argues." *The Denver Post.* No date, 2F.
13 Kavanaugh, Philip. *Magnificent Addiction.* Lower Lake, California: Aslan Publishing, 1992, 115.
14 Durant, Will and Ariel Durant. *The Age of Voltaire.* New York: Simon and Schuster, 1965, 403.
15 May. Rollo. *Man's Search For Himself.* New York: Norton 1953, 42.
16 Ibid, 121.
17 Campbell, Joseph. *The Hero's Journey.* New York: Harper, 1990, 66.
18 Holmes, Ernest. *This Thing Called You.* New York: G. P. Putnam's Sons, 1948, 10.

CHAPTER 6 – The Point of Power Practice
1   Aurelius, Marcus. *The Meditations of Marcus Aurelius.* New York: Avon, 1993, 18.
2   Wilber, Ken, et. al. *Transformations of Consciousness.* Boston: Shambhala Publications, Inc., 1986, 229.

3   Roberts, Jane. *The Nature of Personal Reality.* New York: Bantam, 1974, ix-xi.
4   Ibid, 46.
5   Wilber, Ken, et. al. *Transformations of Consciousness.* Boston: Shambhala Publications, Inc., 1986, 259-260 and 265.

CHAPTER 7 – Response and Reaction
1   Wilber, Ken, et. al. *Transformations of Consciousness.* Boston: Shambhala Publications, Inc., 1986, 156.
2   Chopra, Deepak. *The Seven Spiritual Laws of Success.* San Rafael: Amber-Allen Publishing, 1994, 41.
3   Aurelius, Marcus. *The Meditations of Marcus Aurelius.* New York: Avon, 1993, 74.
4   Jung, C. G. *The Portable Jung.* New York: Penguin Books, 1971, 547.
5   Belitsos, Byron. "Neurotechnology's Shadow." *Shift: At the Frontiers of Consciousness.* Petaluma, California, September-November, 2007, 20.
6   Nisker, Wes. "The Dharma and The Drama." *Inquiring Mind.* Barre, MA. (No date), 46.
7   Chopra, Deepak. *The Seven Spiritual Laws of Success.* San Rafael: Amber-Allen Publishing, 1994, 57.
8   Roberts, Jane. *The Nature of Personal Reality.* New York: Bantam, 1974, 108.
9   Aurelius, Marcus. *The Meditations of Marcus Aurelius.* New York: Avon, 1993, 14-15.
10 Ibid, 56.
11 Armstrong, Karen. "Compassions Fruit." *AARP The Magazine.* March/April, 2005, 64.
12 Tolle, Eckhart. http://www.eckharttolle.com/home/

CHAPTER 8 – Intuition and Intellect
1   Gibran, Kahlil. *The Prophet.* New York: Knopf, 1923, 54.

CHAPTER 9 – Feelings and Emotions
1   Stevens, Wallace. *The Necessary Angel.* New York: Knopf, 1942, 169.
2   Rinpoche, Sakyong Mipham. "A Reign of Goodness." Shambhala *Sun,* Boulder, Colorado, September, 2005, 15.
3   Gyatso, Tenzin. *The Dalai Lama: A Policy of Kindness.* New York: Snow Lion Publications, 1990, 95.
4   Rinpoche, Dzongsar Khyentse. "Buddhism in a Nutshell." *Shambhala Sun.* Boulder, Colorado, March (no year), 41.

5   Johnson, Clive, *Vedanta. An Anthology of Hindu Scripture, Commentary, and Poetry.* New York: Bantam, 1971, 134.

6   Kato, Kay Mieno. *Buddhism for Everyday Living.* Denver: McGraw Printery, 1968, 35.

7   Harvey, Andrew. *The Essential Mystics.* San Francisco: Harper, 1998, 130.

8   Will, George. "America's conservative core runs broad and deep." *The Denver Post.* October 10, 2004, 7E.

9   Roberts, Jane. *The Nature of Personal Reality.* New York: Bantam, 1974, 12-13.

10   Teasdale, Wayne. *The Mystic Heart.* Novato, California: New World Library, 1999, 59.

11   Troward, Thomas. *Bible Mystery and Bible Meaning.* New York: Dodd, 1913, 102-103.

12   O'Connor, Colleen. "Needed: a revolution of the heart." *The Denver Post.* March 20, 2005, 9L.

13   Matousek, Mark. "Stroke of Luck." *AARP Journal,* November/December, 2008, 24.

14   Institute of Noetic Sciences. "The 2008 Shift Report." *Shift: At the Frontier of Consciousness."* Petaluma, March-May 2008, 64-65.

15   Campbell, Joseph. *Creative Mythology.* New York: Viking, 1968, 652.

16   Jung, C. G. *Abstracts of the Collected Works of C. G. Jung.* Rockville, Maryland: NIMH, 1978, 114.

17   Johnson, Robert. *He: Understanding Masculine Psychology.* New York: Harper, 1989, 36.

18   Davis, Thomas D. *Philolosophy.* New York: McGraw-Hill, 1993, 66.

19   Harpur, Tom. *The Pagan Christ.* New York: Walker and Company, 2004, 47.

20   Wilber, Ken. *Sex, Ecology and Spirituality.* Boston: Shambhala Publications Inc., 1995, 307.

21   Troward, Thomas. *The Edinburgh Lectures on Mental Science.* New York: Dodd, 1909, 56.

22   Harrison, Steven. *Doing Nothing.* New York: Tarcher/Putnam, 1997, 84-85.

CHAPTER 10 – Paradigm B (P-B)

1   Russell, Peter. *Waking Up in Time.* Novato, California: Origin Press, 1992, 91.

2   Johnson, Clive, *Vedanta. An Anthology of Hindu Scripture, Commentary, and Poetry.* New York: Bantam, 1971, 98.

3 Roberts, Jane. *The Nature of Personal Reality.* New York: Bantam, 1974, 31.
4 Fox, Emmet. *The Sermon on the Mount.* New York: Harper, 1934, 19.
5 May, Rollo. *The Discovery of Being.* New York: W.W. Norton and Company. 1983, 118.
6 Van der Post, Laurens. *Jung and the Story of our Time.* New York: Random House, 1975, 134.
7 Streett, Bill. "Science and the Reenchantment of the Cosmos: The Rise of the Integral Vision of Reality." *Shift: At the Frontiers of Consciousness.* Petaluma, California, June-August 2006, 42.
8 Sahtouris, Elisabet. "Seven Reasons Why I Remain an Optimist." *Shift: At the Frontiers of Consciousness.* Petaluma, California, June-August, 2006, 35.
9 Ibid, 36.
10 Wilber, Ken. *Sex, Ecology and Spirituality.* Boston: Shambhala Publications Inc., 1995, 206.
11 Institute of Noetic Sciences. "The 2008 Shift Report." *Shift: At the Frontier of Consciousness."* Petaluma, March-May 2008, 8.
12 Wilber, Ken, et. al. *Transformations of Consciousness.* Boston: Shambhala Publications, Inc., 1986, 88-89.
13 Moore, Thomas. *Dark Nights of the Soul.* New York: Gotham, 2004, 64.
14 Ibid, 205.
15 Roberts, Jane. *The Nature of Personal Reality.* New York: Bantam, 1974, 33.
16 Ibid, 47.
17 Barasch, Marc Ian. "You Are Not My Enemy." *Shift to the Frontiers of Consciousness.* Petaluma, California, June-August, 2005, 27.
18 Foundation For Inner Peace. *A Course in Miracles Volume Three: Manual For Teachers.* Farmingdale, New York: Coleman Graphics, 1975, 28.
19 Van der Post, Laurens. *Jung and the Story of our Time.* New York: Random House, 1975, 20-21.
20 May, Rollo. *The Discovery of Being.* New York: W.W. Norton and Company. 1983, 213.
21 Sugrue, Thomas. *There Is a River.* New York: Holt, 1942, 379.

CHAPTER 11 – Paradigm A (P-A)
1 Johnson, Clive, *Vedanta. An Anthology of Hindu Scripture, Commentary, and Poetry.* New York: Bantam, 1971, 129.

2. Wilber, Ken, et. al. *Transformations of Consciousness.* Boston: Shambhala Publications, Inc., 1986, 116.
3. Van der Post, Laurens. *Jung and the Story of our Time.* New York: Random House, 1975, 147.
4. Institute of Noetic Sciences. "The 2008 Shift Report." *Shift: At the Frontier of Consciousness."* Petaluma, March-May 2008, 35.
5. Ibid, 41.
6. Wilber, Ken, et. al. *Transformations of Consciousness.* Boston: Shambhala Publications, Inc., 1986, 227.
7. Jung, C. G. *The Portable Jung.* New York: Penguin Books, 1971, 604.
8. Troward, Thomas. *The Edinburgh Lectures on Mental Science.* New York: Dodd, 1909, 99.
9. Campbell, Joseph. *Hero With a Thousand Faces.* New York: Bollingen Foundation, Inc., 1949, 16-17.
10. Gibran, Kahlil. *The Prophet.* New York: Knopf, 1923, 38.
11. Ibid, 17.
12. Siegel, Bernie S. *Love, Medicine and Miracles.* New York: Harper, 1986, 82-83.
13. Durant, Will. *Our Oriental Heritage.* New York: Simon and Schuster, 1954, 415.
14. Ibid, 413.
15. Ibid, 413.
16. Ibid, 415.
17. Ibid, 410.
18. Ibid, 436.
19. Ibid, 412.
20. Ibid, 412.
21. Smith, A. Robert, "Medicine's 'Magic Bullets' Miss the Mark." *Venture Inward.* July/August, 1993, 31.

CHAPTER 12 – Paradigm Shift
1. Sheehan, Thomas. *The First Coming.* New York: Random House, 1986, 63.
2. Murck, Christian, ed. *Artists and Traditions: Uses of the Past in Chinese Culture.* Princeton, New Jersey, Princeton University Press, 1976, 185.
3. Harsanyi, David. "Don't stress on stress." *The Denver Post.* November 6, 2009, 11B.
4. Roberts, Jane. *The Nature of Personal Reality.* New York: Bantam, 1974, 53-57.

5   Ibid, 71.
6   Feinstein, David. "Subtle Energy: Psychology's Missing Link." *IONS Noetic Review,* Petaluma, California, June-August, 2003, 32.
7   Porterfield, Christopher. "Duel at the Tipping Point." *Time.* March 14, 2005, 62.
8   Johnson, Robert. *Transformation.* San Francisco: Harper, 1991, 83.
9   Willis Harman in Institute of Noetic Sciences. *The 2007 Shift Report.* 2007, frontispiece.
10   Johnson, Robert. *Transformation.* San Francisco: Harper, 1991, 82-83.
11   May, Rollo. "Creativity." *Shift: At the Frontiers of Consciousness.* Petaluma, California, March-May 2005, 37.
12   Campbell, Joseph. *The Power of Myth.* New York: Bantam, 1988, 126.
13   Troward, Thomas. *The Edinburgh Lectures on Mental Science.* New York: Dodd, 1909, 74-85.
14   Editor. "The New Paradigm of Connectedness." *Shift: At the Frontiers of Consciousness.* Petaluma, California, March-May, 2006, 8.
15   Wilber, Ken. *Sex, Ecology and Spirituality.* Boston: Shambhala Publications Inc., 1995, 267.
16   Ibid, 276.
17   Institute of Noetic Sciences. "The 2008 Shift Report." *Shift: At the Frontier of Consciousness."* Petaluma, March-May 2008, 58-64.
18   Hibbard, Addison, and Horst Frenz. *Writers of the Western World.* New York: Houghton, 1954, 762.
19   May. Rollo. *Man's Search For Himself.* New York: Norton 1953, 153.
20   Ibid, 77.
21   Wilber, Ken, et. al. *Transformations of Consciousness.* Boston: Shambhala Publications, Inc., 1986, 268.
22   Rinpoche, Chogyam Trungpa. *Illusion's Game.* Boston: Shambhala, 1994, 50-51.
23   May. Rollo. *Man's Search For Himself.* New York: Norton 1953, 160.
24   Sinetar, Marsha. *Ordinary People as Monks and Mystics.* New York: Paulist Press, 1986, 112.
25   Foundation For Inner Peace. *A Course in Miracles Volume Three: Manual For Teachers.* Farmingdale, New York: Coleman Graphics, 1975, 79.
26   Campbell, Joseph. *The Power of Myth.* New York: Bantam, 1988, 112.
27   Sheehan, Thomas. *The First Coming.* New York: Random House, 1986, 254.
28   Van Auken, John. [ed.] "In Our Womb of Consciousness." *Personal Spirituality.* June/July 2009, 1-2.

29 Foundation For Inner Peace. *A Course in Miracles Volume Three: Manual For Teachers.* Farmingdale, New York: Coleman Graphics, 1975, 28.

CHAPTER 13 – Meditation

1. Gunaratana, Henepola. *Mindfulness in Plain English.* Boston: Wisdom Publications. 1991, 77.
2. Hart, William. *Vipassana Meditation as Taught by S. N. Goenka.* San Francisco: Harper, 1987, 78.
3. Fischer, Zoketsu Norman. "The Universal Technique of S. N. Goenka." *Shambhala Sun.* Boulder, Colorado, September, 2001, 50.
4. Wilber, Ken, et. al. *Transformations of Consciousness.* Boston: Shambhala Publications, Inc., 1986, 17.
5. Lawrence, Mac. "The Search for a Nonviolent Future." *Timeline.* November/December, 2002, 8.
6. Troward, Thomas. *The Edinburgh Lectures on Mental Science.* New York: Dodd, 1909, 93.
7. Rahula, Walpola. *What the Buddha Taught.* New York: Grove Weidenfeld, 1959, 68.
8. Ibid, 68-69.
9. Rinpoche, Sakyong Mipham. "A Reign of Goodness." *Shambhala Sun,* Boulder, Colorado, September, 2005, 16.
10. Lama, Dalai, His Holiness, The. "Contemplative Mind: Hard Science." *Shift: At the Frontiers of Consciousness.* Petaluma, California, December 2005—February, 2006, 26-28.
11. Boyce, Barry. "Two Sciences of Mind." *Shambhala Sun,* Boulder, Colorado, September, 2005, 94.
12. Wilber, Ken, et. al. *Transformations of Consciousness.* Boston: Shambhala Publications, Inc., 1986, 266-267.
13. Hawkins, David. *The Eye of the I.* Sedona, Arizona: Veritas Publishing, 2001, 83-84.
14. Ibid, 85-86.
15. Wilber, Ken, et. al. *Transformations of Consciousness.* Boston: Shambhala Publications, Inc., 1986, 20-21.
16. Ibid, viii-ix.
17. Hahn, Thich Nhat. "For 30 Years the Best Buddhism in America: Meditation." *Shambhala Sun.* January 2010, 67.
18. Aurelius, Marcus. *The Meditations of Marcus Aurelius.* New York: Avon, 1993, 12.

19 Bennett, *Venture Inward,* Virginia Beach: Association for Research and Enlightenment, January/ February, 2007, 48.
20 Ferrucci, Piero. *Inevitable Grace.* Los Angeles: Tarcher, 1990, 111.
21 Boyce, Barry. "Overcoming Shyness; Mindful Divorce." *Shambhala Sun.* January, 2002, 79.
22 Wilber, Ken, et. al. *Transformations of Consciousness.* Boston: Shambhala Publications, Inc., 1986, 158.
23 Ibid, 140, 153 and 168.
24 Rinpoche, Dilgo Khentse. "The Mind's True Nature." *Shambhala Sun.* Boulder, Colorado, January, 2009, 77.
25 Campbell, Joseph. *The Hero's Journey.* New York: Harper, 1990, 214.

CHAPTER 14 – Present Moment
1 Emerson, Ralph Waldo. *The Portable Emerson.* New York: Viking, 1946, 123.
2 Hutchins, Robert Maynard [ed.], *Great Books of the Western World: The Great Ideas: A Syntopicon Vol. I.* Encyclopedia Britannica, Inc. 1952, 438.
3 Ross, David. "The Light Enters You." *Shambhala Sun,* Boulder, Colorado, November, 2004, 49.
4 Russell, Peter. *Waking Up in Time.* Novato, California: Origin Press, 1992, 93.
5 Ibid, 93.
6 Rinpoche, Tulka Urgyen. "Existence & Nonexistence." *Shambhala Sun.* Boulder, Colorado, March, 2000, 63.
7 Gunaratana, Henepola. *Mindfulness in Plain English.* Boston: Wisdom Publications. 1991, 152-153.
8 Roberts, Jane. *The Nature of Personal Reality.* New York: Bantam, 1974, 292.
9 Johnson, Clive, *Vedanta. An Anthology of Hindu Scripture, Commentary, and Poetry.* New York: Bantam, 1971, 151.
10 Packer, Toni. "Toni Packer." *Shambhala Sun.* Boulder, Colorado, July, 2005, 46.
11 Tolle, Eckhart. *A New Earth.* New York: Dutton, 2005, 241.
12 Ferguson, Gaylon. "Evaluating Eckhart." *Shambhala Sun.* Boulder, Colorado, July, 2008, 87.
13 Wilber, Ken. *Sex, Ecology and Spirituality.* Boston: Shambhala Publications Inc., 1995, 295.
14 Campbell, Joseph. *The Hero's Journey.* New York: Harper, 1990, 148.

15 Braden, Charles S. *Spirits in Rebellion: The Rise and Development of New Thought.* Dallas: Southern Methodist University Press, 1987, 135.
16 Adam, Michael. *Wandering in Eden: Three Ways to the East Within Us.* New York: Knopf, 1976, 67.
17 Wilber, Ken. *Sex, Ecology and Spirituality.* Boston: Shambhala Publications Inc., 1995, 505-506.
18 Ibid, 523.
19 Powell, Diane. "We Are All Savants." *Shift: At the Frontiers of Consciousness.* Petaluma California, December 2005-February 2006, 17.
20 Tauber, Alfred. *Henry David Thoreau and the Moral Agency of Knowing.* Los Angeles: University of California Press, 2001, 15.
21 Wilber, Ken. *Sex, Ecology and Spirituality.* Boston: Shambhala Publications Inc., 1995, 303.
22 May. Rollo. *Man's Search For Himself.* New York: Norton 1953, 228.
23 Wilber, Ken, et. al. *Transformations of Consciousness.* Boston: Shambhala Publications, Inc., 1986, 271.

CHAPTER 15 – Peak Experience
1 Sinetar, Marsha. *Ordinary People as Monks and Mystics.* New York: Paulist Press, 1986, 108-109.
2 Roberts, Jane. *The Nature of Personal Reality.* New York: Bantam, 1974, 197.
3 Ferrucci, Piero. *Inevitable Grace.* Los Angeles: Tarcher, 1990, 59.
4 Ardagh, Arjuna. "Cultivating Translucence." *Shift at the Frontiers of Consciousness.* Petaluma, September-November, 2005, 29.
5 Ferrucci, Piero. *Inevitable Grace.* Los Angeles: Tarcher, 1990, 245.
6 Brome, Vincent. *Jung: Man and Myth.* New York: Atheneum, 1981, 228.
7 Jung, C. G. *Abstracts of the Collected Works of C. G. Jung.* Rockville, Maryland: NIMH, 1978, 107.
8 Edinger, Edward. *The Creation of Consciousness: Jung's Myth for Modern Man.* Toronto, Canada: Inner City Books, 1984, 81.
9 Sinetar, Marsha. *Ordinary People as Monks and Mystics.* New York: Paulist Press, 1986, 98.

CHAPTER 16 – Silence, Simplicity, Solitude
1 Gibran, Kahlil. *The Prophet.* New York: Knopf, 1923, 60.
2 Brome, Vincent. *Jung: Man and Myth.* New York: Atheneum, 1981, 263.
3 Gibran, Kahlil. *The Prophet.* New York: Knopf, 1923, 60.

4   Emerson, Ralph Waldo. *The Portable Emerson.* New York: Viking, 1946, 192.
5   Pearce, Joseph Chilton. "Evolution's End." *Science of Mind.* Los Angeles: June, 1993, 35.
6   Aurelius, Marcus. *The Meditations of Marcus Aurelius.* New York: Avon, 1993, 26.
7   Magill, Frank N. ed. *Masterpieces of World Literature.* New York: Harper, 1989, 726.

CHAPTER 17 – Absolute and Relative
1   Wilber, Ken. "Letters." *What is Enlightenment?* Lennox, Massachusetts, Spring/Summer, 1999, 8.
2   Rinpoche, Dzogchen Ponlop. "The Wisdom of the Body and the Search for the Self." *Shambhala Sun.* Boulder, Colorado, September, 2004, 59.
3   Rahula, Walpola. *What the Buddha Taught.* New York: Grove Weidenfeld, 1959, 39.
4   Johnson, Clive, *Vedanta. An Anthology of Hindu Scripture, Commentary, and Poetry.* New York: Bantam, 1971, 220.
5   Ibid, 212.
6   Bays, Jan Chozen. "Ultimately You're Healthy Relatively You Die." *Shambhala Sun,* Boulder, Colorado, May 2005, 40.
7   Cohen, Andrew and Ken Wilber. "the Guru and the Pandit, Following the Grain of the Kosmos dialog V." *What is Enlightenment?* Lennox, Massachusetts, May-July, 2004, 46.
8   Foundation For Inner Peace. *A Course in Miracles Volume Three: Manual For Teachers.* Farmingdale, New York: Coleman Graphics,1975, 4.
9   Hartmann, Thom. *The Last Hours of Ancient Sunlight.* Northfield, Vermont: Mythic, 1998, 50.
10 Yogis, Jaimal. "Ride of a Lifetime." *Shambhala Sun.* Boulder, Colorado, March, 2006, 29.
11 Teasdale, Wayne. *The Mystic Heart.* Novato, California: New World Library, 1999, 52.
12 Braden, Charles S. *Spirits in Rebellion: The Rise and Development of New Thought.* Dallas: Southern Methodist University Press, 1987, 38.

CHAPTER 18 – Transcendence
1   Cohen, Andrew and Ken Wilber. "the Guru and the Pandit, Following the Grain of the Kosmos dialog V." *What is Enlightenment?* Lennox, Massachusetts, May-July, 2004, 47.

2 Miller, Arthur. *All My Sons, et. al.* New York: Penguin Books, 1995, 379.
3 Moore, Thomas. *Dark Nights of the Soul.* New York: Gotham, 2004, 24.
4 Wilber, Ken. "Letters." *What is Enlightenment?* Lennox, Massachusetts, Spring/Summer, 1999, 8.
5 Ibid, 9.
6 Jung, C. G. *Abstracts of the Collected Works of C. G. Jung.* Rockville, Maryland: NIMH, 1978, 46.
7 Roberts, Jane. *The Nature of Personal Reality.* New York: Bantam, 1974, 157.
8 Johnson, Clive, *Vedanta. An Anthology of Hindu Scripture, Commentary, and Poetry.* New York: Bantam, 1971, 259.
9 Capra, Fritjof. *The Tao of Physics.* New York: Bantam, 1975, 14.
10 Kabat-Zinn, Jon. *Wherever You Go, There You Are.* New York: Hyperion, 1994, 32.
11 Roberts, Jane. *The Nature of Personal Reality.* New York: Bantam, 1974, 293.
12 Rinpoche, Sakyong Mipham. "Seeing the Essence of Phenomena as Wisdom." *Shambhala Sun.* Boulder, Colorado, May, 2004, 46.

CHAPTER 19 – Fear

1 Gibran, Kahlil. *The Prophet.* New York: Knopf, 1923, 49.
2 Kavanaugh, Philip. *Magnificent Addiction.* Lower Lake, California: Aslan Publishing, 1992, 101.
3 Seldes, George. *The Great Thoughts.* New York: Random House, 1985, 252.
4 Edinger, Edward. *The Creation of Consciousness: Jung's Myth for Modern Man.* Toronto, Canada: Inner City Books, 1984, 63.
5 Williamson, Marianne. *A Return to Love.* New York: Harper Collins, 1992, 19.
6 Foundation For Inner Peace. *A Course in Miracles Volume Three: Manual For Teachers.* Farmingdale, New York: Coleman Graphics, 1975, 39.
7 Tolle, Eckhart. http://www.eckharttolle.com/news-4htm
8 May, Rollo. *Man's Search For Himself.* New York: Norton 1953, 38.
9 Gaylin, Willard. *Adam and Eve and Pinocchio:On Being and Becoming Human.* New York: Penguin, 1990, 135.
10 Kavanaugh, Philip. *Magnificent Addiction.* Lower Lake, California: Aslan Publishing, 1992, 220.

11 May, Rollo. *The Discovery of Being*. New York: W.W. Norton and Company. 1983, 109.
12 Ferrucci, Piero. *Inevitable Grace*. Los Angeles: Tarcher, 1990, 294.
13 Fox, Matthew. *Original Blessings*. Sante Fe: Bear and Company, 1983, 82.
14 Troward, Thomas. *Collected Essays of Thomas Troward*. Marina Del Rey, CA: De Vorss and Company, 1921, 27.
15 Squires, James. "Campaign '92.' *The Denver Post*. June 23, 1992.

CHAPTER 20 – Compassion
1 Roberts, Jane. *The Nature of Personal Reality*. New York: Bantam, 1974, 145.
2 Ibid, 145.
3 Ibid, 146.
4 Borysenko, Joan. *Guilt is the Teacher, Love is the Lesson*. New York: Warner, 1990, 95.

CHAPTER 21 – Implicate Order
1 Smith, A. Robert, "Science discovers the Akashic field." *Venture Inward*. July/August, 2008, 46.
2 Parry, Glenn Aparicio. "Native Wisdom in a Quantum World." *Shift: At the Frontier of Consciousness*. Petaluma, California, December 2005–February 2006, 32.
3 Streett, Bill. "Science and the Reenchantment of the Cosmos: The Rise of the Integral Vision of Reality." *Shift: At the Frontiers of Consciousness*. Petaluma, California, June-August 2006, 42.
4 DeQuincy, Christian. "Multimedia." *Shift: At the Frontier of Consciousness*. Petaluma, California, March-May 2005.
5 Fields, Rick. *Chop Wood, Carry Water*. Los Angeles: Tarcher, 1984, 207.
6 Keepin, Will. "Science and Spirit: Integrating the Sacred and the Secular." *Timeline*. Palo Alto, September/October, 1998, 4.
7 Ibid, 2.
8 Ibid, 2-4.
9 Brome, Vincent. *Jung: Man and Myth*. New York: Atheneum, 1981, 221.
10 Jung, C.G. *Man and His Symbols*. New York: Doubleday, 1964, 38.
11 Aurelius, Marcus. *The Meditations of Marcus Aurelius*. New York: Avon, 1993, 35.
12 Ibid, 52.

13. Emerson, Ralph Waldo. *The Portable Emerson.* New York: Viking, 1946, 371.
14. Roberts, Jane. *The Nature of Personal Reality.* New York: Bantam, 1974, 396-399.
15. Ibid, 125.
16. Troward, Thomas. *The Edinburgh Lectures on Mental Science.* New York: Dodd, 1909, 48.
17. Troward, Thomas. *Bible Mystery and Bible Meaning.* New York: Dodd, 1913, 6-7.
18. Errico, Rocco A. *Let There Be Light.* Marina del Rey, California: Devorss & Company, 1985, xviii.
19. Fox Matthew. *The Coming of the Cosmic Christ.* New York: Harper, 1988, 194.
20. Holmes, Fenwick L. *Ernest Holmes: His Life and Times.* New York: Dodd, Mead, & Company, 1970, 171.
21. Holmes, Ernest. *The Science of Mind.* New York: Dodd, Mead & Company, 1938, 348-349.
22. Chopra, Deepak. "The Healing Reality." *Science of Mind.* Los Angeles, November, 1989, 17.
23. Ibid, 21.
24. Rinpoche, Chogyam Trungpa. "Reflections in the Cosmic Mirror." *Shambhala Sun.* Boulder, Colorado, January 2009, 76.

CHAPTER 22 – The Algebra of Simple Reality
1. Durant, Will. *Our Oriental Heritage.* New York: Simon and Schuster, 1954, 428-429.
2. Ibid, 429.
3. Ferrucci, Piero. *Inevitable Grace.* Los Angeles: Tarcher, 1990, 97-98.
4. Ibid, 108.

CHAPTER 23 – Right View
1. Boyce, Barry. "Mind, Matter, or God" *Shambhala Sun, Boulder, Colorado,* January, 2008, 53.
2. Freemantle, Francesca. "Another Reality." *Shambhala Sun.* Boulder, Colorado, November, 2004, 55.
3. Johnson, Clive, *Vedanta. An Anthology of Hindu Scripture, Commentary, and Poetry.* New York: Bantam, 1971, iv.
4. Roberts, Jane. *The Nature of Personal Reality.* New York: Bantam, 1974, ix-xi.
5. Ibid, 46.

6   Johnson, Charles. "The King We Need." *Shambhala Sun.* Boulder, Colorado, January, 2005, 50.
7   Phipps, Carter. "No escape for the ego." *What is Enlightenment?* Lennox, Massachusetts, Spring/Summer, 2000, 55.
8   Johnson, Clive, *Vedanta. An Anthology of Hindu Scripture, Commentary, and Poetry.* New York: Bantam, 1971, 91.
9   Ibid, 120.
10 Ibid, 131.
11 Ibid, 218.
12 Cohen, Andrew and Ken Wilber. "the Guru and the Pandit, Breaking the Rules." *What is Enlightenment?* Lennox, Massachusetts, Fall/Winter, 2002, 48.
13 Cohen, Andrew and Ken Wilber. "the Guru and the Pandit, Breaking the Rules." *What is Enlightenment?* Lennox, Massachusetts, Fall/Winter, 2002, 48.
14 Edinger, Edward. *The Creation of Consciousness: Jung's Myth for Modern Man.* Toronto, Canada: Inner City Books, 1984, 9.
15 Ibid, 9.
16 Ibid, 9-10.
17 Ibid, 62.
18 Ibid, 63.
19 Roberts, Jane. *The Nature of Personal Reality.* New York: Bantam, 1974, 166.
20 Edinger, Edward. *The Creation of Consciousness: Jung's Myth for Modern Man.* Toronto, Canada: Inner City Books, 1984, 62.
21 Rinpoche, Dzogchen Ponlop. "What the Buddha Taught." *Shambhala Sun.* Boulder, Colorado, May, 2006, 103.

CHAPTER 24 – Collective Unconscious
1   Wilber, Ken. *A Brief History of Everything.* Boston: Shambhala, 1996, 213.
2   Guiley, Rosemary Ellen. *Harper's Encyclopedia of Mystical and Paranormal Experience.* San Francisco: Harper, 1991, 114.
3   Roberts, Jane. *The Nature of Personal Reality.* New York: Bantam, 1974, 13-14.
4   Ibid, 41.
5   Ibid, 45.
6   Jung, C. G. *The Portable Jung.* New York: Penguin Books, 1971, 103.
7   Jung, C. G. *Abstracts of the Collected Works of C. G. Jung.* Rockville, Maryland: NIMH, 1978, 65.

8. Jung, C. G. *The Portable Jung.* New York: Penguin Books, 1971, 103.
9. Jung, C. G. *Abstracts of the Collected Works of C. G. Jung.* Rockville, Maryland: NIMH, 1978, 51.

CHAPTER 25 – Buddha and Christ

1. Smith, Huston. *The Religions of Man.* New York: Harper, 1958, 99.
2. Unno, Taitetsu. "The Power of Negative Thinking." *Shambhala Sun,* Boulder, Colorado, July, 2001, 86.
3. Rinpoche, Shyalpa. "A Path of Honesty." *Shambhala Sun.* Boulder, Colorado, May, 2003, 37.
4. Rinpoche, Dzogchen Ponlop. "What the Buddha Taught." *Shambhala Sun.* Boulder, Colorado, May, 2006, 53.
5. Russell, Peter. *Waking Up in Time.* Novato, California: Origin Press, 1992, 97.
6. Rinpoche, Dzogchen Ponlop. "What the Buddha Taught." *Shambhala Sun.* Boulder, Colorado, May, 2006, 46.
7. Fisher, Zoketsu Norman. "Coming Home to the Body." *Shambhala Sun.* Boulder, Colorado, July, 2008, 69.
8. Harpur, Tom. *The Pagan Christ.* New York: Walker and Company, 2004, 166.
9. Ibid, 161-165.
10. Ibid, 45.
11. Ibid, 169.
12. Ibid, 3.
13. Sheehan, Thomas. *The First Coming.* New York: Random House, 1986, 190-191.
14. Roberts, Jane. *The Nature of Personal Reality.* New York: Bantam, 1974, 431.
15. Jung, C. G. *The Portable Jung.* New York: Penguin Books, 1971, 582-583.
16. Ibid, 582-583.
17. Edinger, Edward. *The Creation of Consciousness: Jung's Myth for Modern Man.* Toronto, Canada: Inner City Books, 1984, 84-85.
18. Ibid, 84-85.
19. Ibid, 94.
20. Ibid, 94.
21. Jung, C. G. *Abstracts of the Collected Works of C. G. Jung.* Rockville, Maryland: NIMH, 1978, 61.
22. Ibid, 104.

23 Wilber, Ken. *Sex, Ecology and Spirituality.* Boston: Shambhala Publications Inc., 1995, 350-357.

CHAPTER 26 – Self-Reliance
1 Johnson, Clive, *Vedanta. An Anthology of Hindu Scripture, Commentary, and Poetry.* New York: Bantam, 1971, 217.
2 Ibid, 133.
3 Goenka, S.N. "The Buddha's Path Is For Experiencing Reality." *Vipassana Newsletter.* Vol. 29, No. 1, May, 2002.
4 Rahula, Walpola. *What the Buddha Taught.* New York: Grove Weidenfeld, 1959, 9.
5 Johnson, Clive, *Vedanta. An Anthology of Hindu Scripture, Commentary, and Poetry.* New York: Bantam, 1971, 4.
6 Ibid, 211.
7 Tarrant, John. "Paradox, Breakthrough, and the Zen Koan." *Shift: At the Frontiers of Consciousness.* Petaluma, California, March-May 2005, 26.
8 Campbell, Joseph. *Myths To Live By.* New York: Bantam, 1973, 144.
9 Jung, C. G. *The Portable Jung.* New York: Penguin Books, 1971, 488.
10 Ibid, 486-487.
11 Ibid, 605-606.
12 May. Rollo. *Man's Search For Himself.* New York: Norton 1953, 161-162.
13 Ibid, 161-162.
14 Jung, C. G. *The Portable Jung.* New York: Penguin Books, 1971, 457-459.
15 Moyers, Bill. *Bill Moyers A World of Ideas.* New York: Doubleday, 1989, 421.
16 Ranke-Heinemann. Uta. *Putting Away Childish Things.* New York: Harper/Collins, 1994, 59.
17 Buber, Martin. *Martin Buber's Ten Rungs.* New York: Citadel, 1974, 18.
18 Hutchins, Robert Maynard [ed.], *Great Books of the Western World: Great Ideas: A Syntopicon Vol. I.* Encyclopedia Britannica, Inc. 1952, 417.
19 Peterson, Roland. *Everyone is Right.* Marina del Ray, California: DeVorss and Company, 1986, 205.
20 Roberts, Jane. *The Nature of Personal Reality.* New York: Bantam, 1974, 34-35.

[21] Emerson, Ralph Waldo. *The Portable Emerson.* New York: Viking, 1946, 139.
[22] Tauber, Alfred. *Henry David Thoreau and the Moral Agency of Knowing.* Los Angeles: University of California Press, 2001, 199.
[23] May. Rollo. *Man's Search For Himself.* New York: Norton 1953, 145.
[24] Troward, Thomas. *Bible Mystery and Bible Meaning.* New York: Dodd, 1913, 226-227 and 231.
[25] Peterson, Anita Harkin. "Cayce Principles of Child Guidance." *Venture Inward.* January/February 1991, 38.

Made in the USA
Lexington, KY
29 April 2011